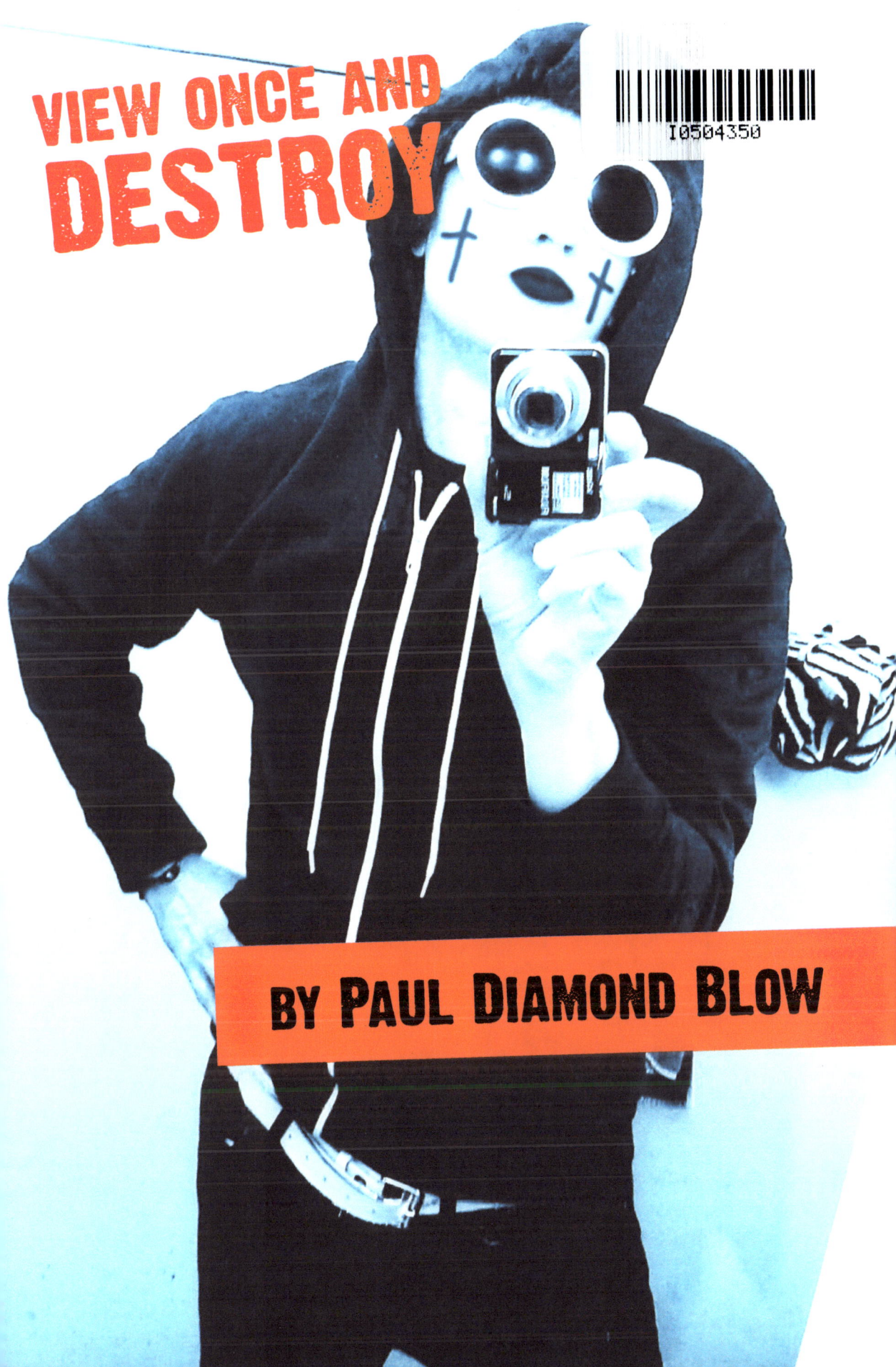

VIEW ONCE AND DESTROY

I0504350

BY PAUL DIAMOND BLOW

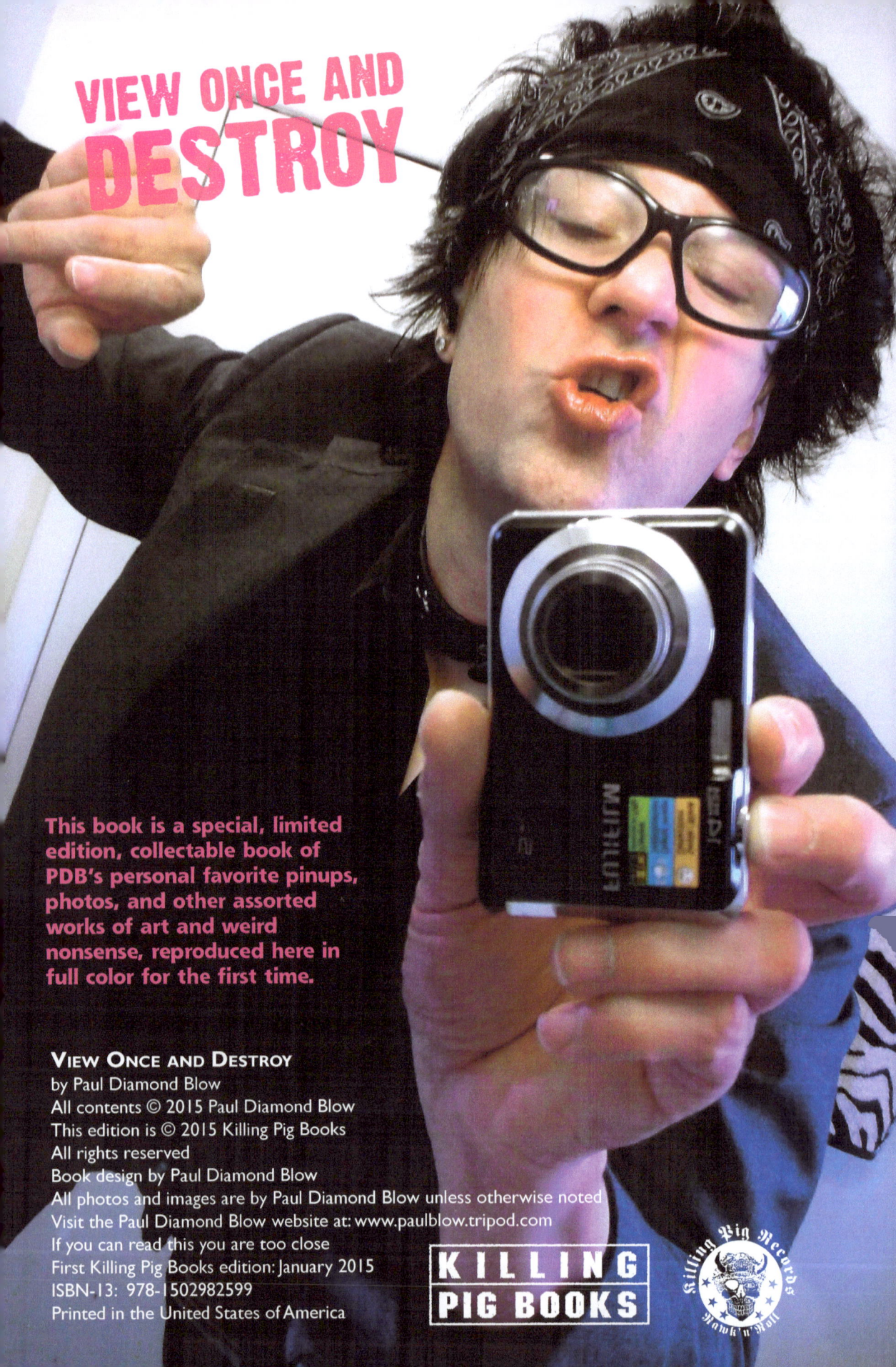

VIEW ONCE AND DESTROY

This book is a special, limited edition, collectable book of PDB's personal favorite pinups, photos, and other assorted works of art and weird nonsense, reproduced here in full color for the first time.

VIEW ONCE and DESTROY

by Paul Diamond Blow
All contents © 2015 Paul Diamond Blow
This edition is © 2015 Killing Pig Books
All rights reserved
Book design by Paul Diamond Blow
All photos and images are by Paul Diamond Blow unless otherwise noted
Visit the Paul Diamond Blow website at: www.paulblow.tripod.com
If you can read this you are too close
First Killing Pig Books edition: January 2015
ISBN-13: 978-1502982599
Printed in the United States of America

KILLING PIG BOOKS

Killing Pig Records · Rawk'n'Roll

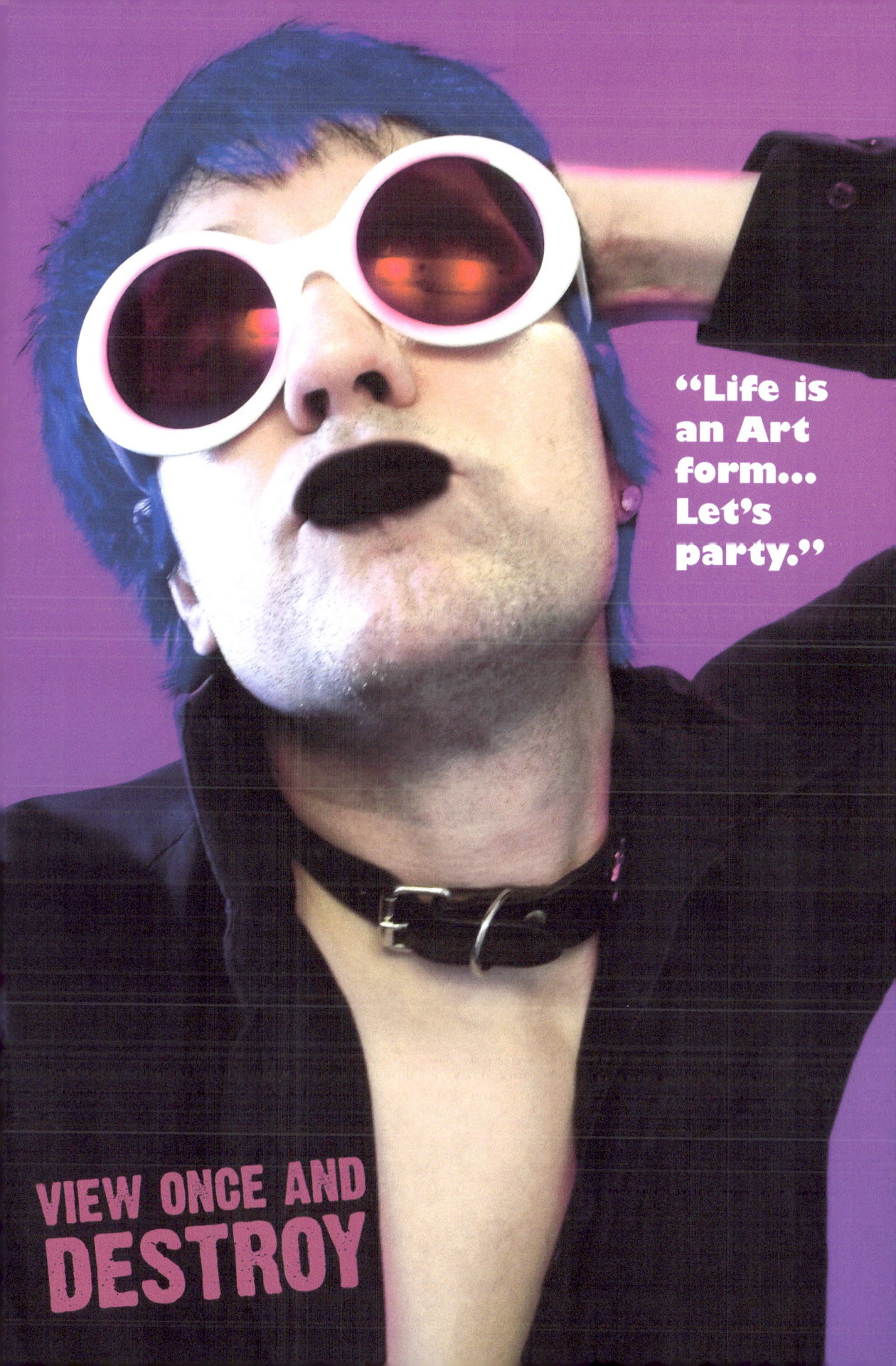

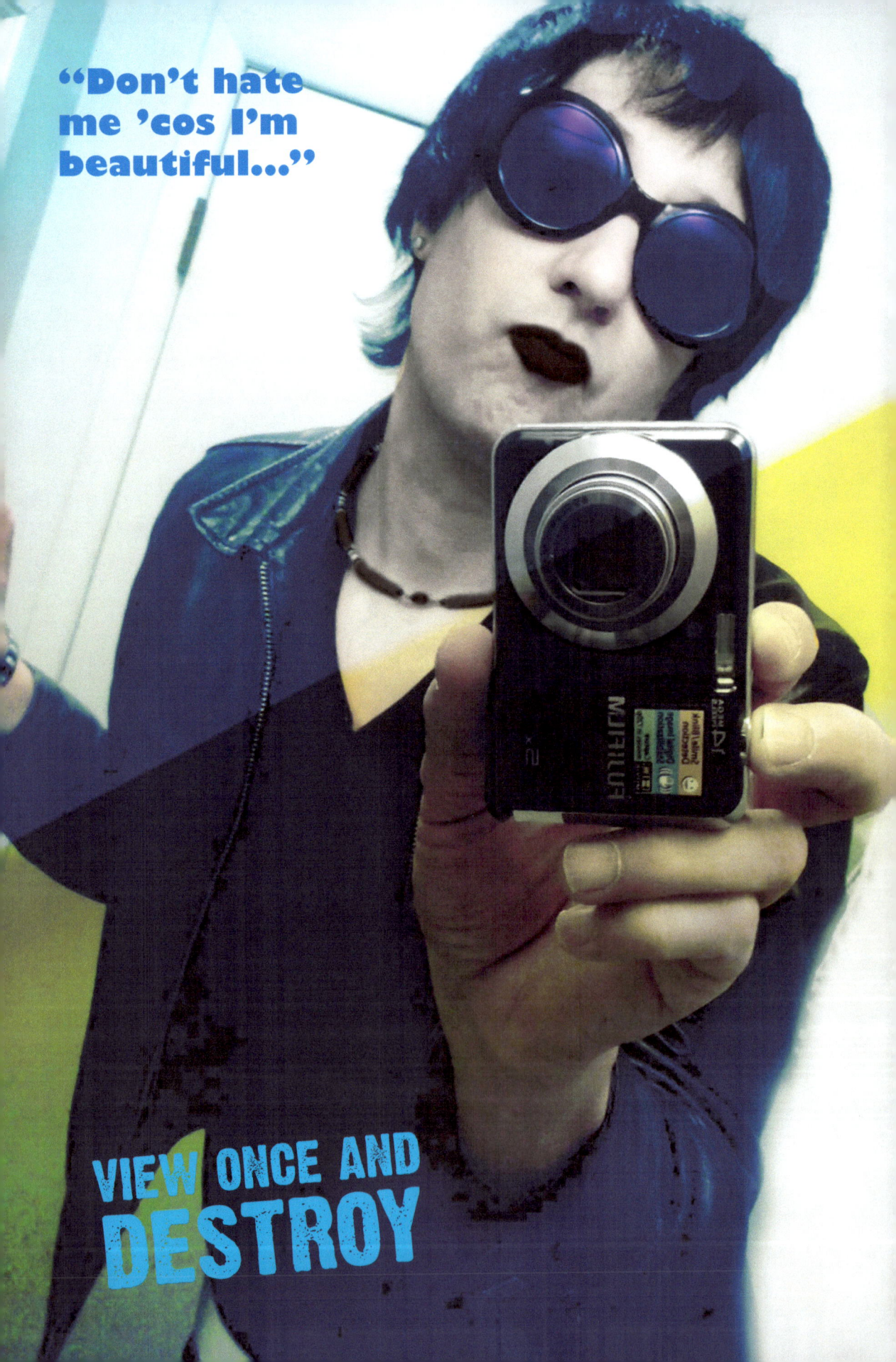

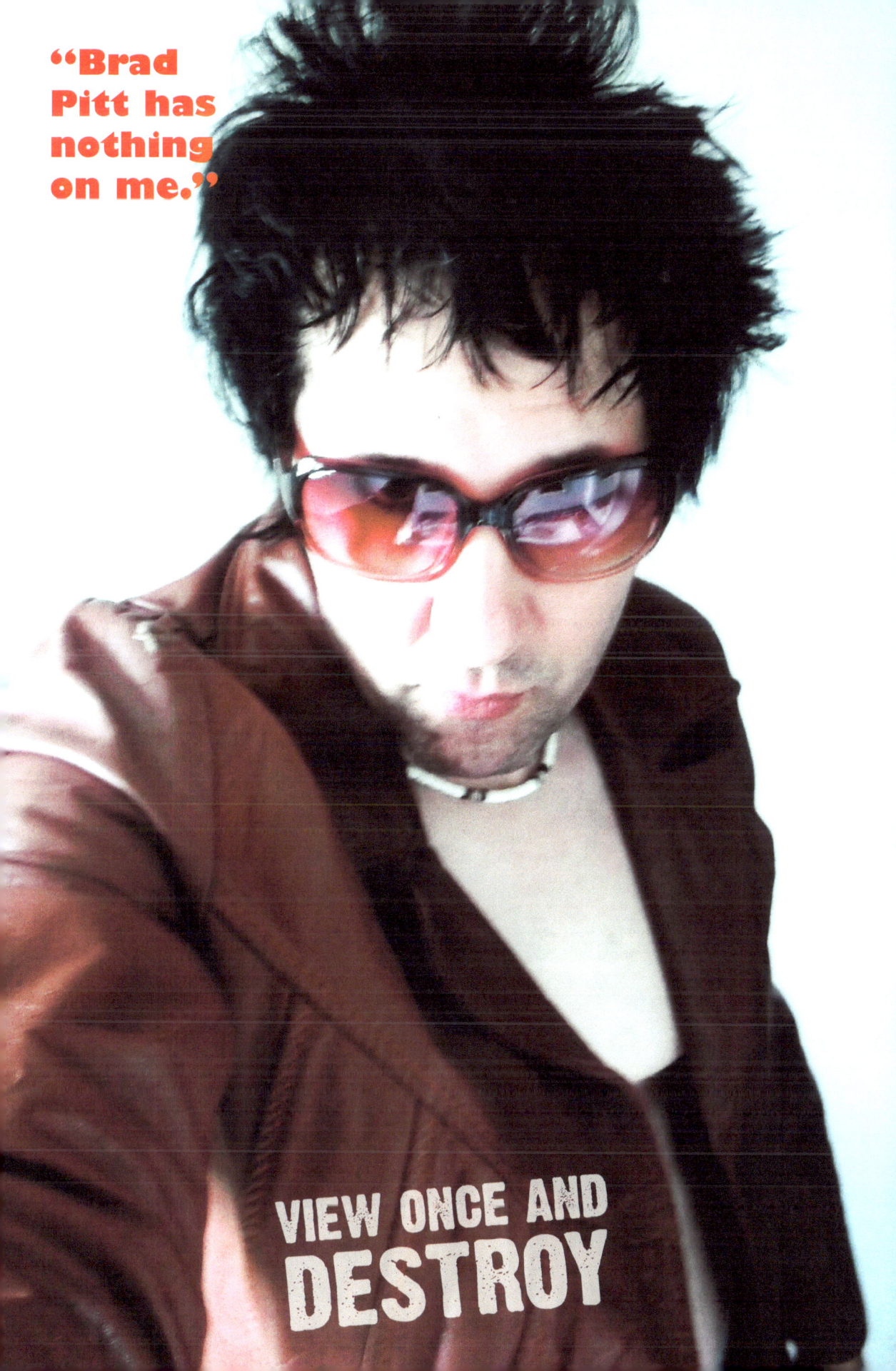

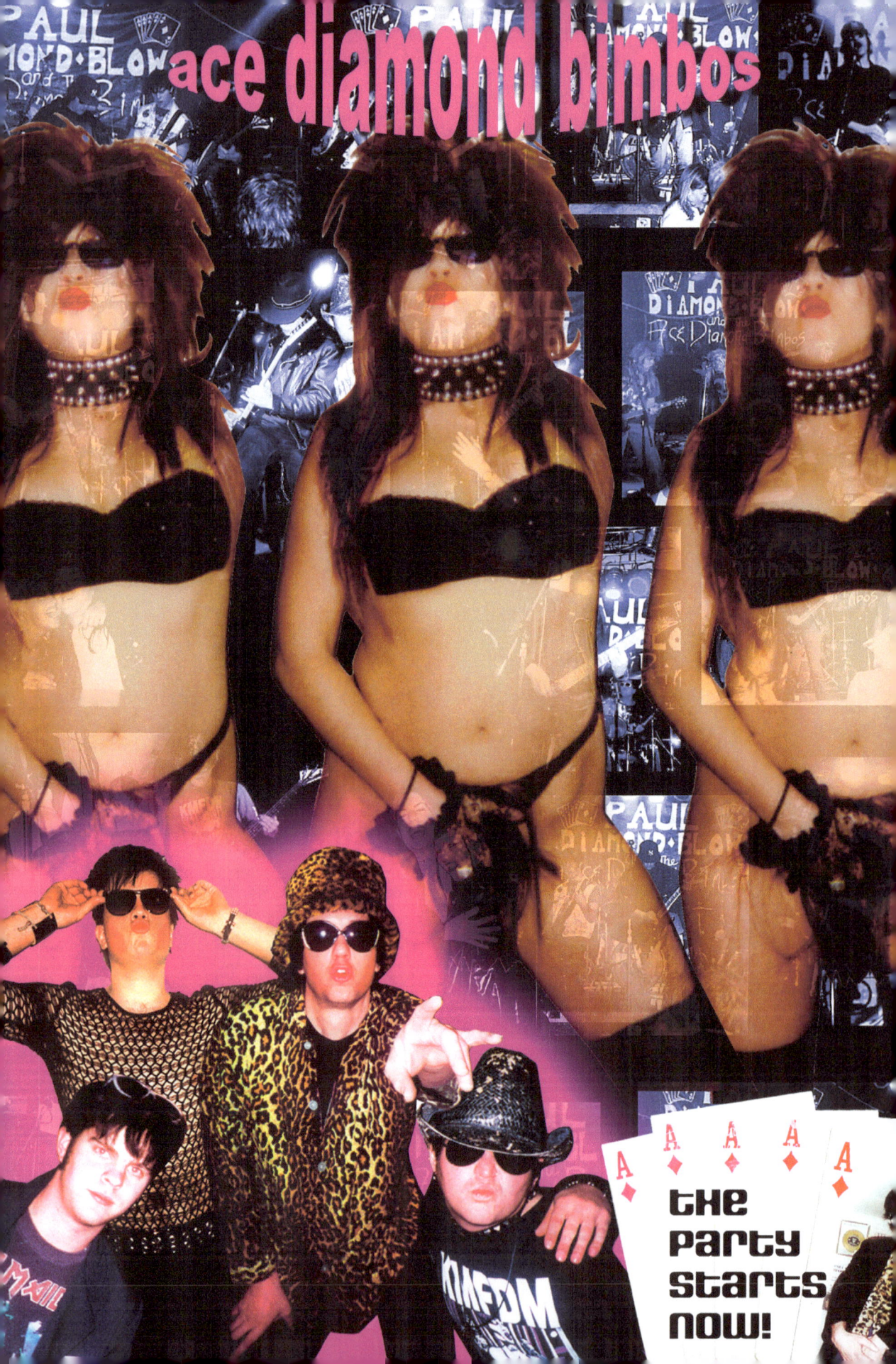

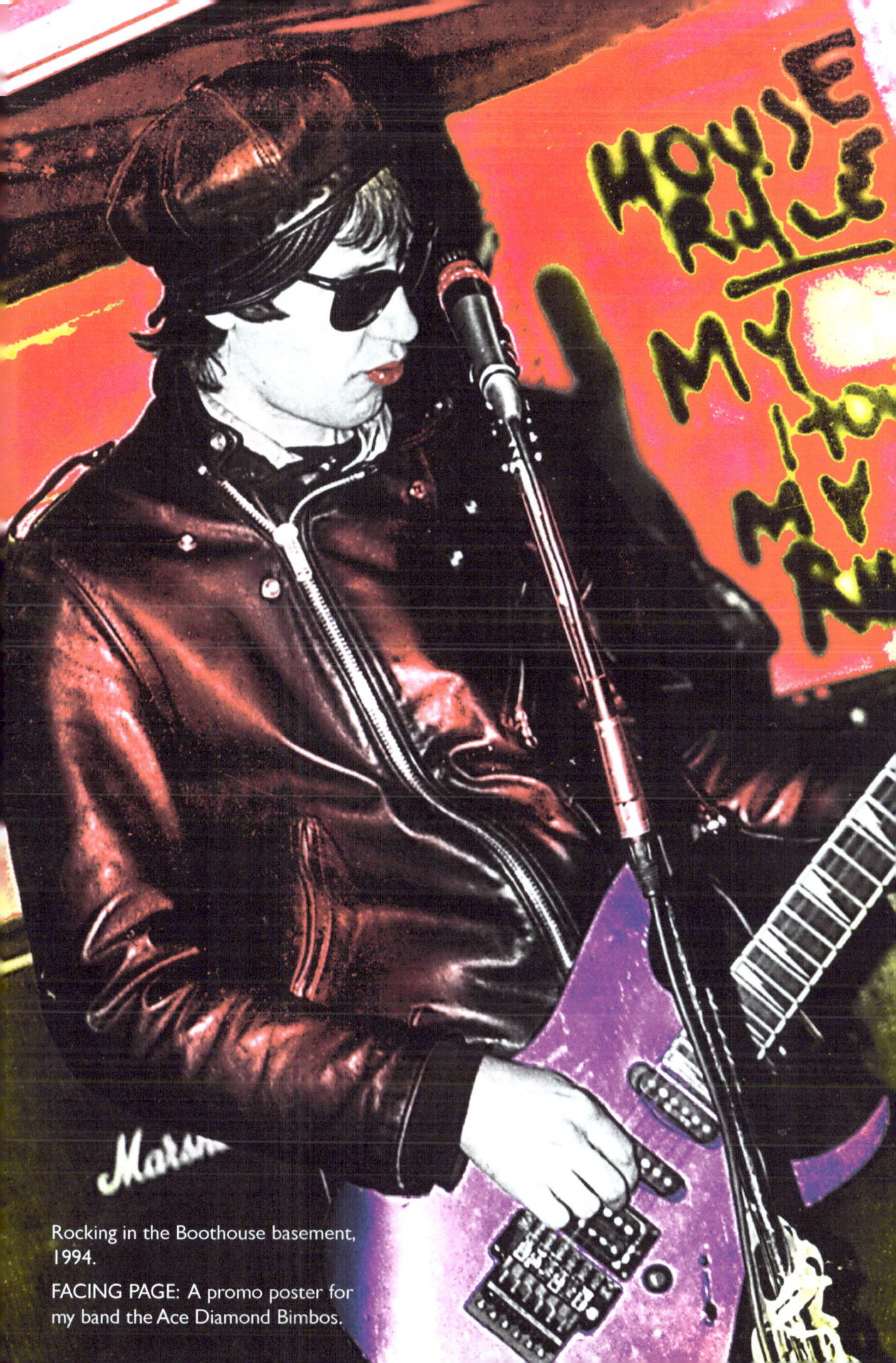

Rocking in the Boothouse basement, 1994.

FACING PAGE: A promo poster for my band the Ace Diamond Bimbos.

JOE MOTOR'S UNDERGROUND PRESENTS:

PAUL DIAMOND BLOW

WITH
JOE MOTOR
AND GUESTS

LIVE IN
CONCERT!

FREE!
NO COVER

FRIDAY, AUGUST 30
BERNARDS (3RD AND SENECA, IN DOWNTOWN SEATTLE)

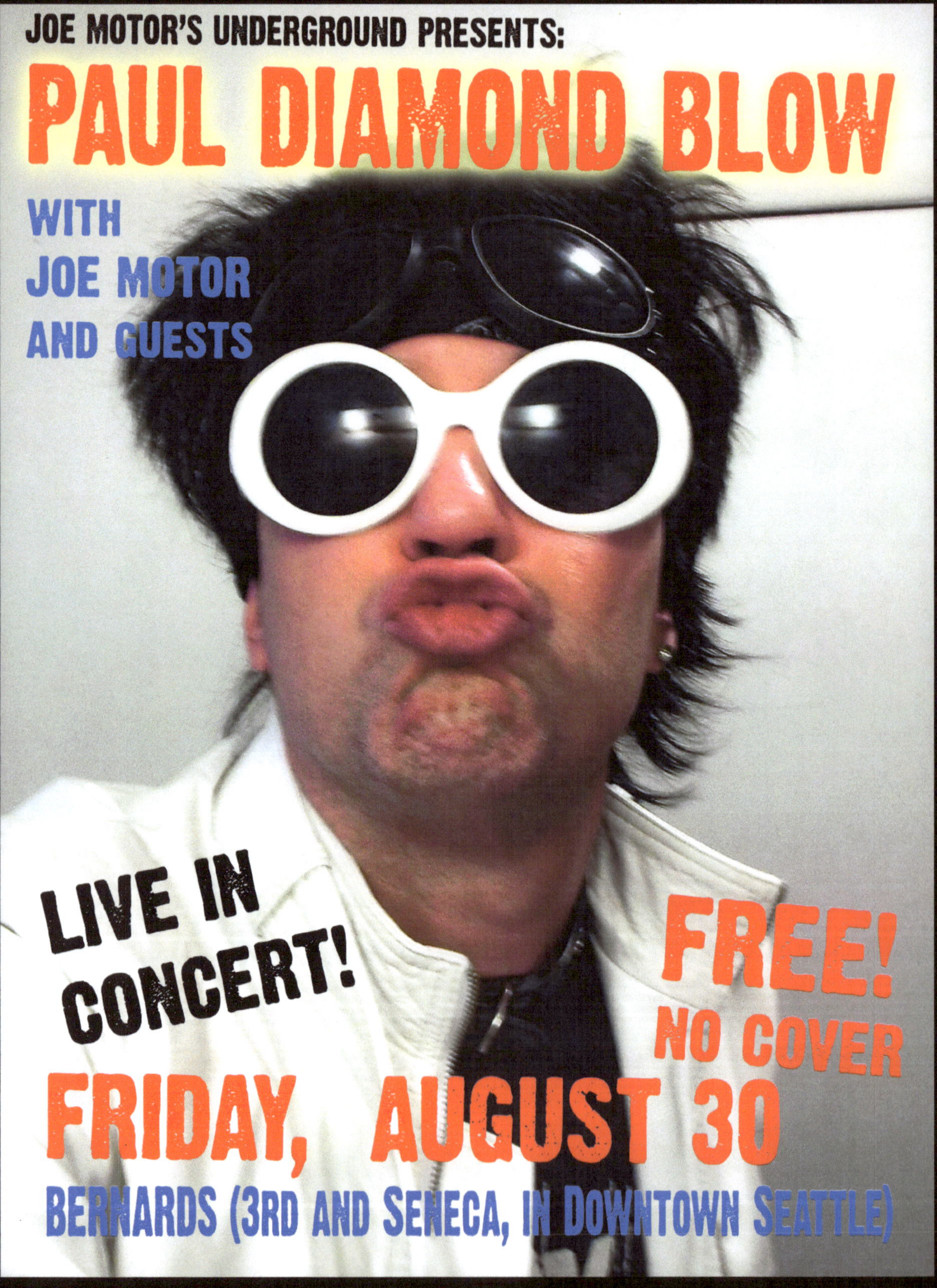

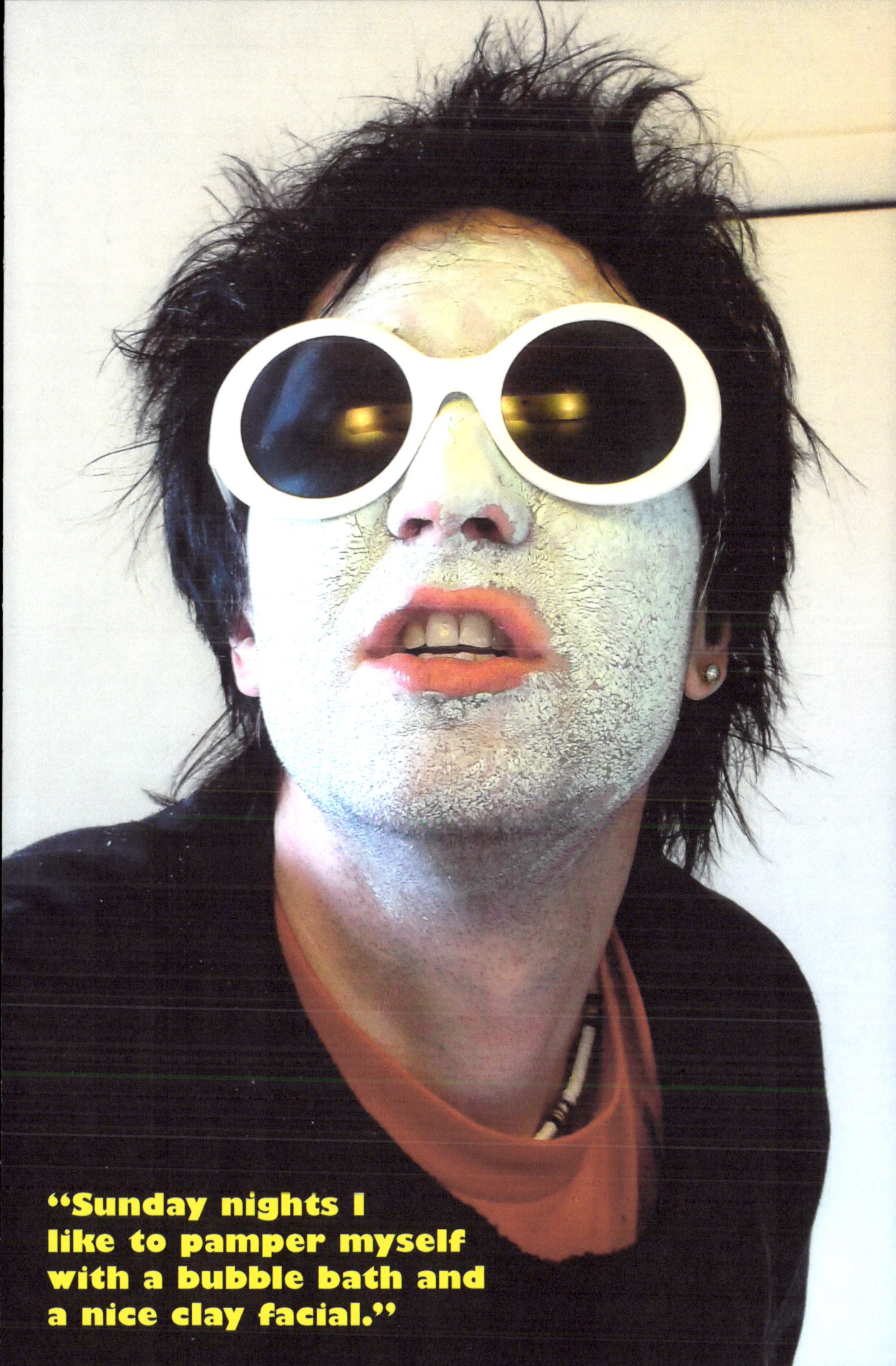

"Sunday nights I like to pamper myself with a bubble bath and a nice clay facial."

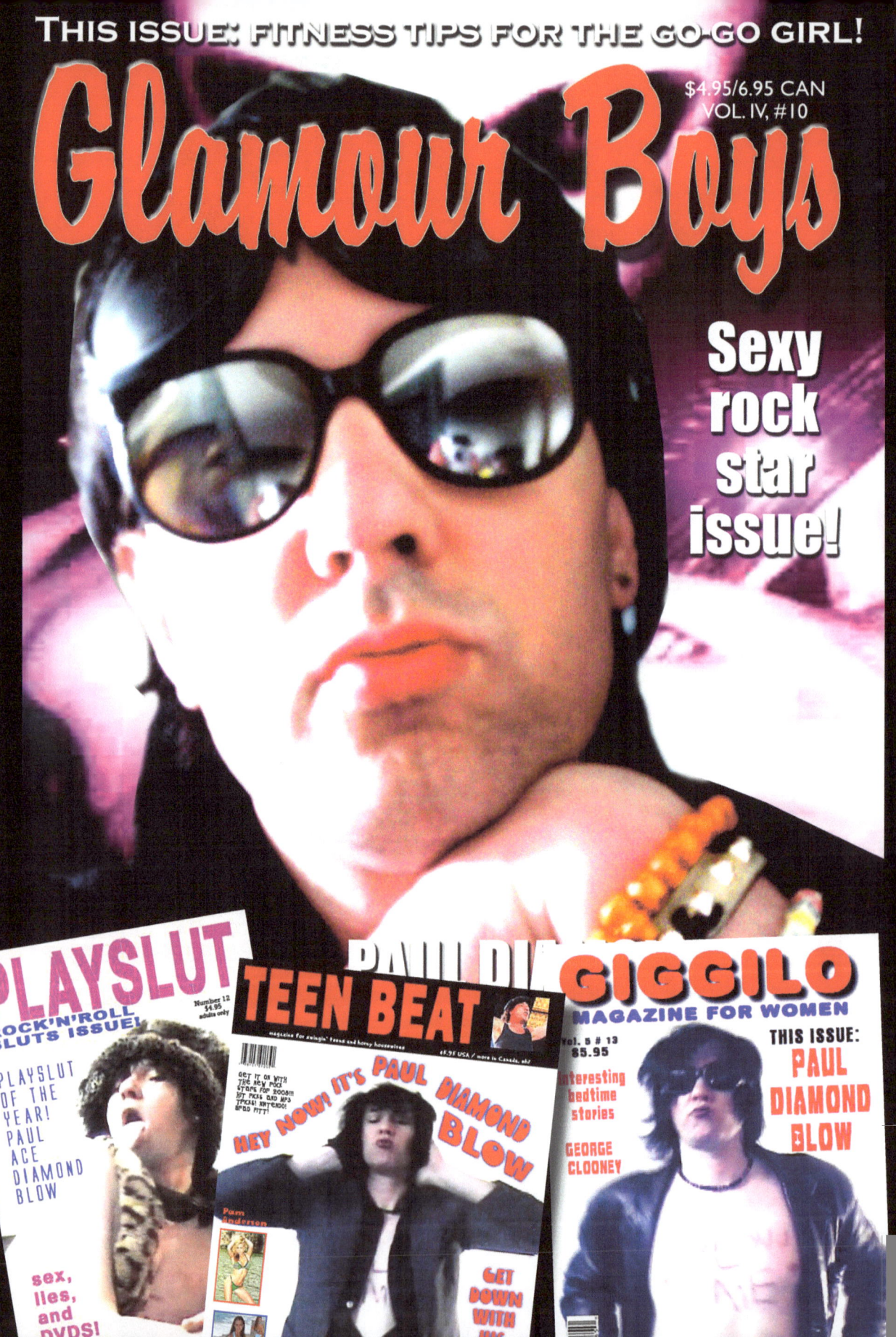

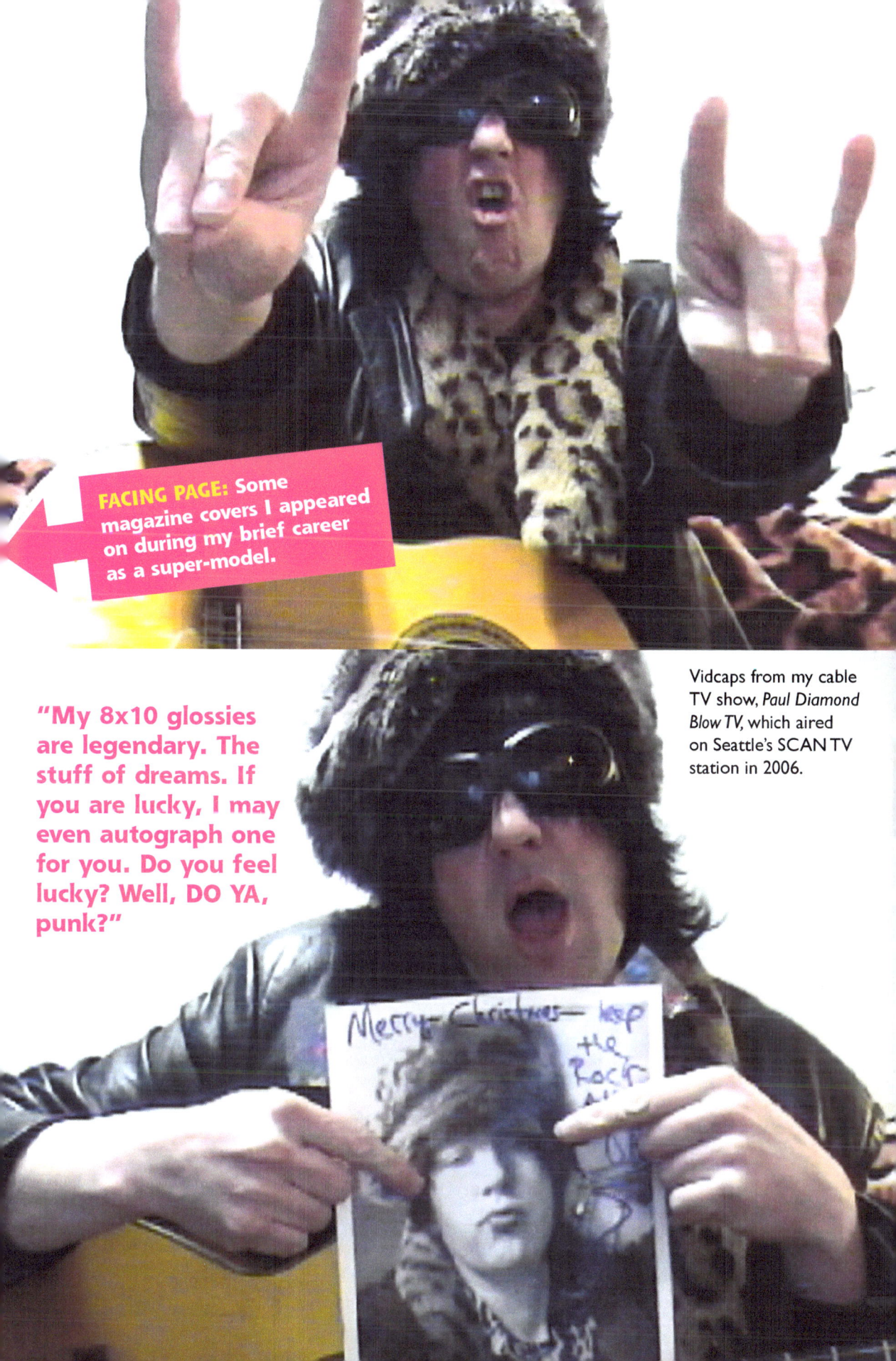

FACING PAGE: Some magazine covers I appeared on during my brief career as a super-model.

"My 8x10 glossies are legendary. The stuff of dreams. If you are lucky, I may even autograph one for you. Do you feel lucky? Well, DO YA, punk?"

Vidcaps from my cable TV show, *Paul Diamond Blow TV*, which aired on Seattle's SCAN TV station in 2006.

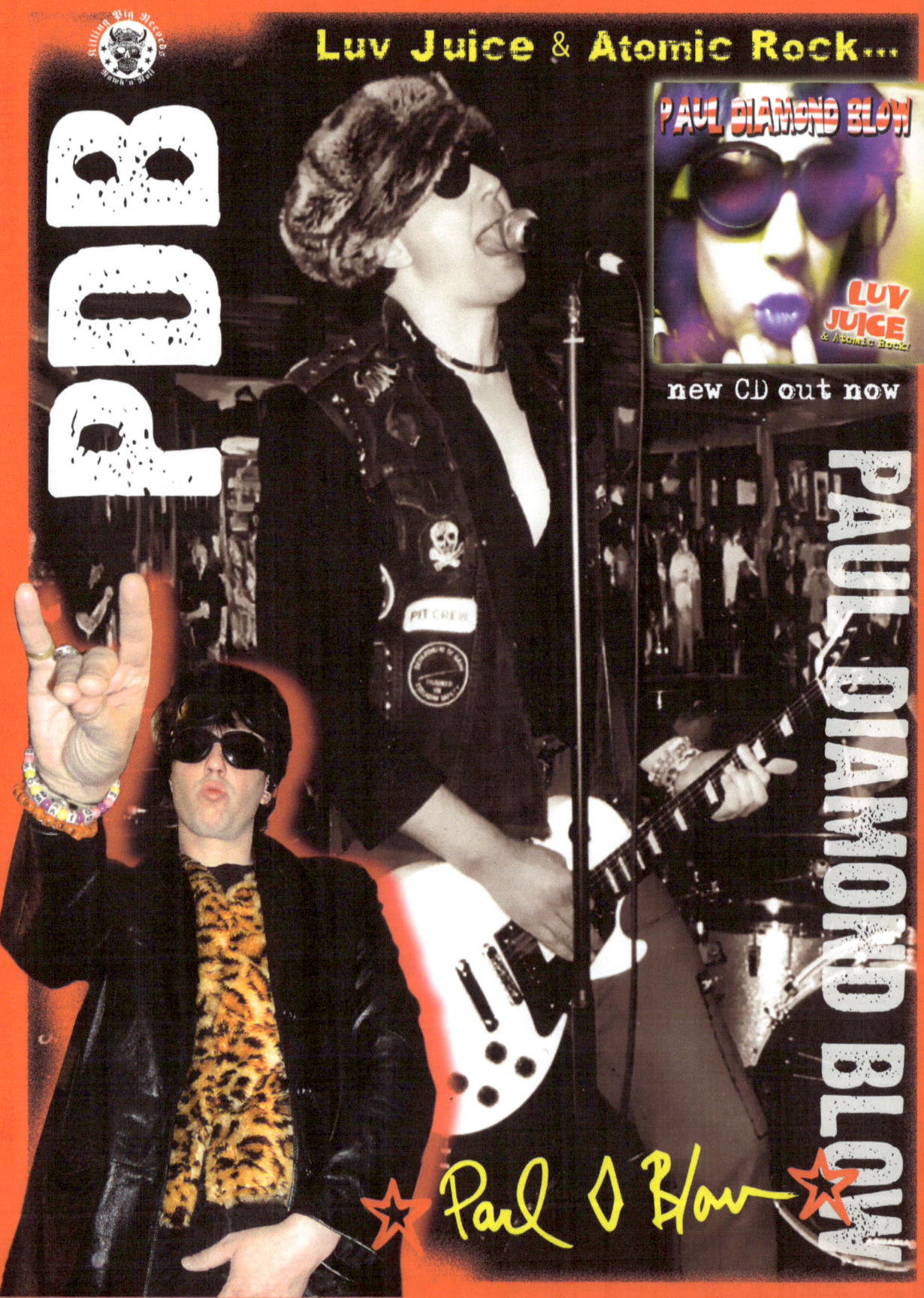

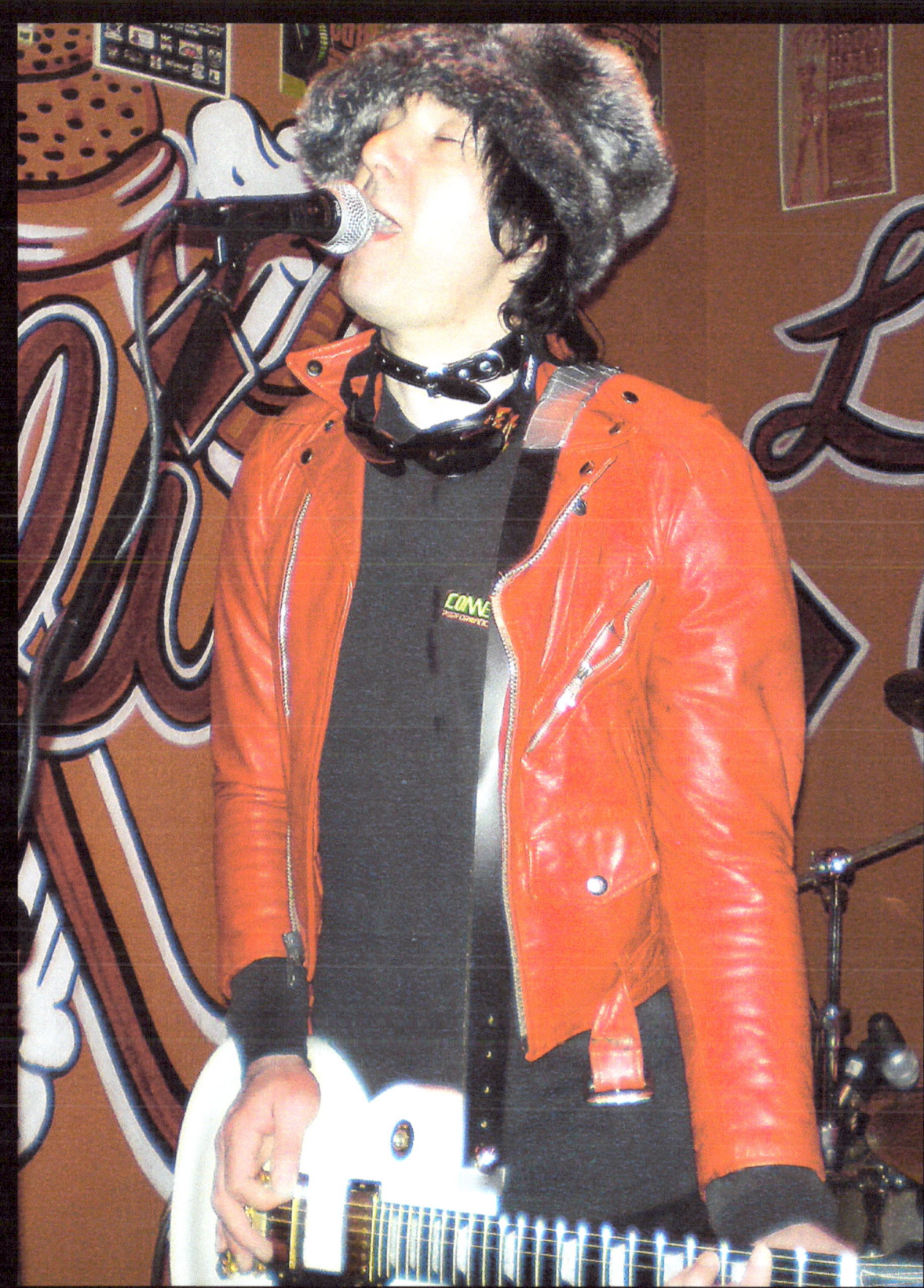

"Nothing says ROCK'N'ROLL like a furry hat, red leather, and a white Les Paul!"

Performing at Slim's Last Chance, 2009

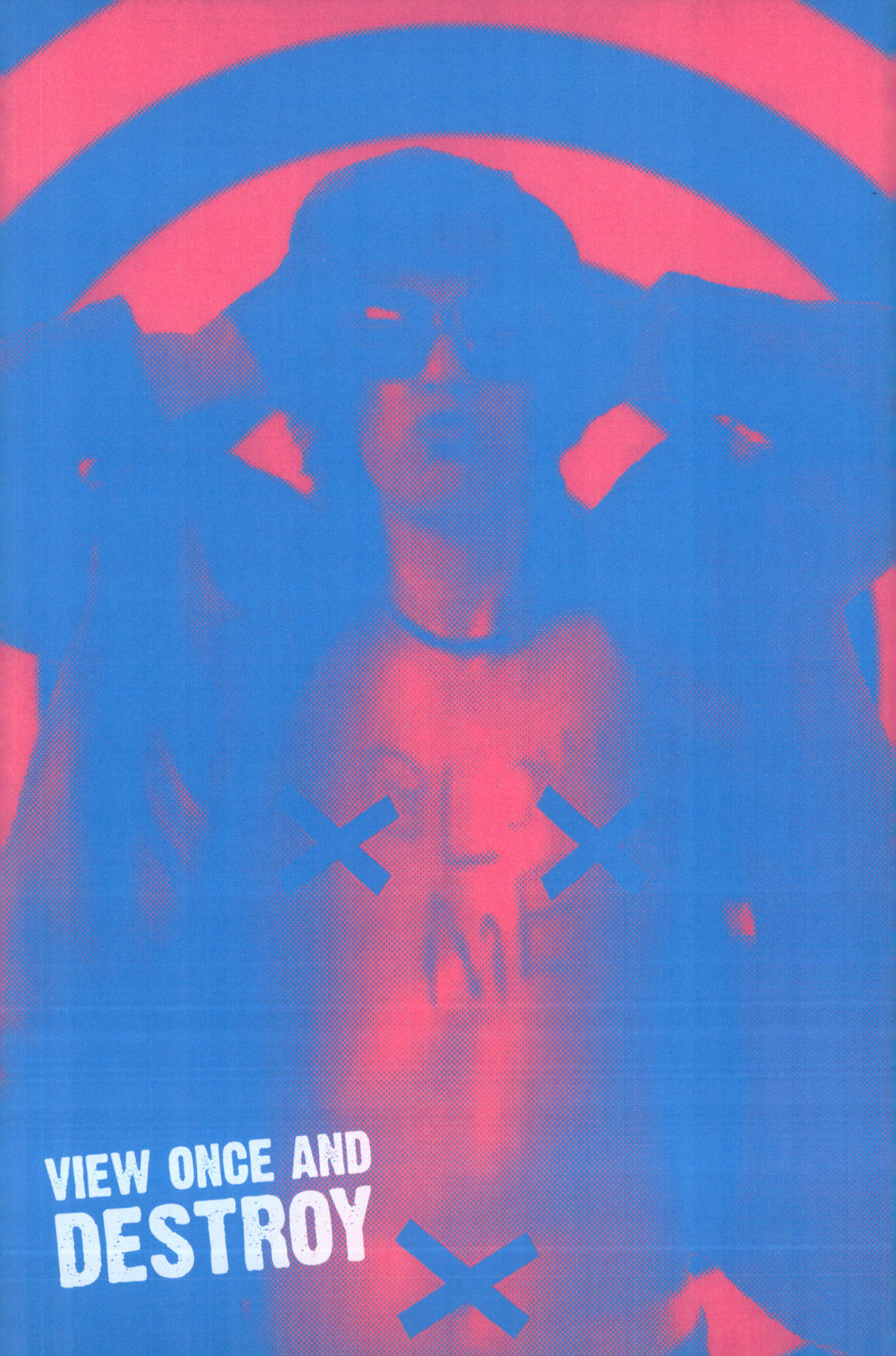

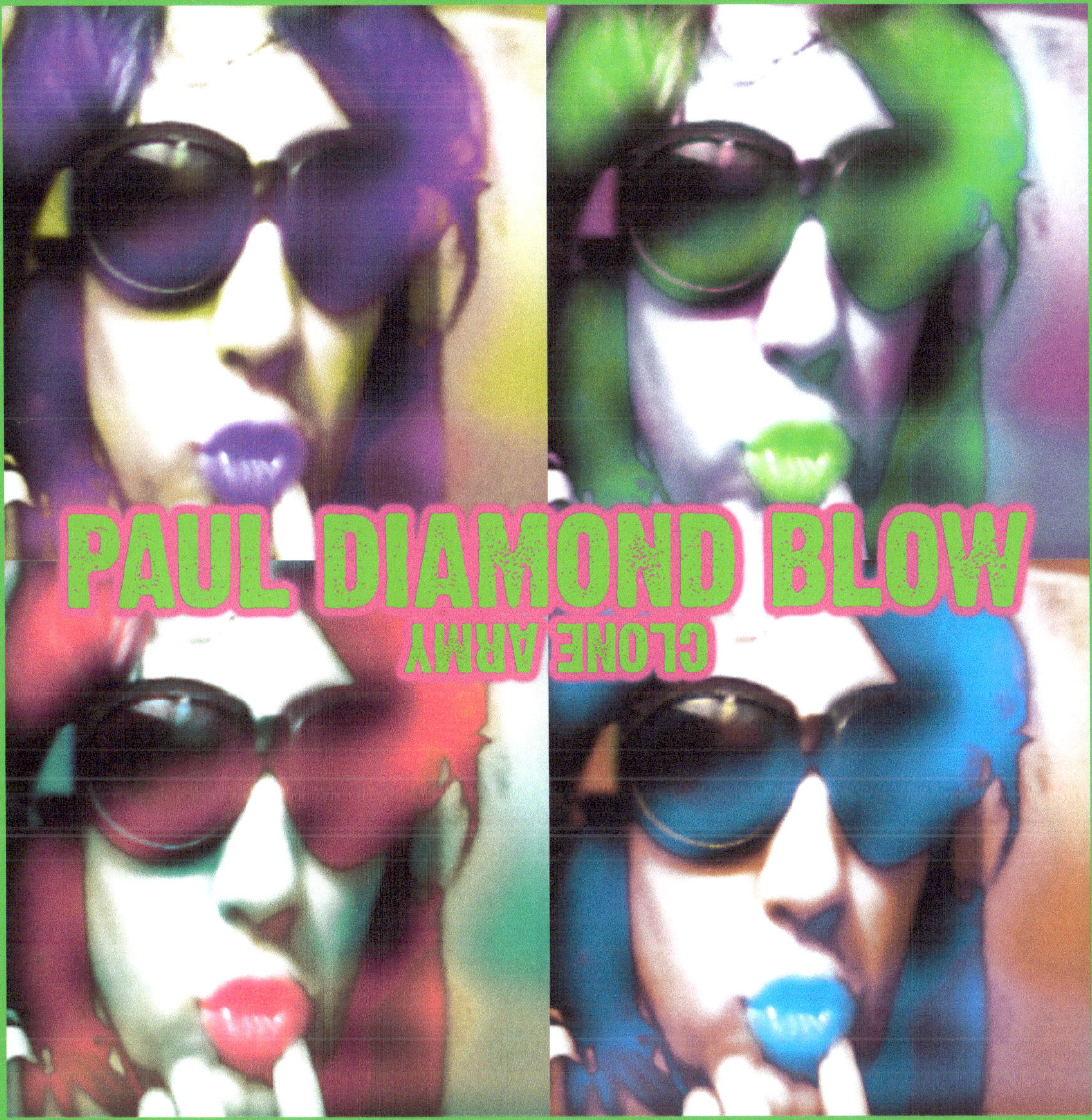

PAUL DIAMOND BLOW
CLONE ARMY

"My ultimate goal is to create a super rock band consisting of clones of myself. Imagine how hard that would ROCK? I would front the band, of course."

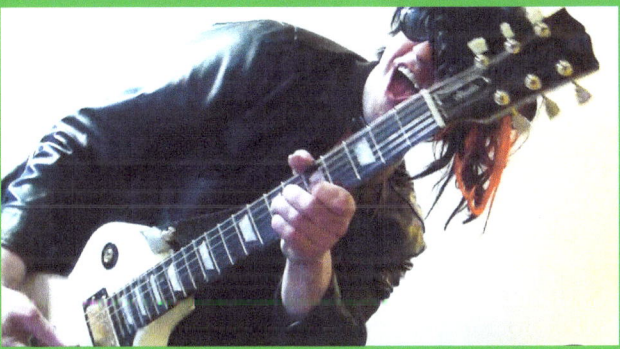

Lipps Diamond rocks the Les Paul

ABOVE: The CD cover for my next solo album, which will feature my Clone Army backing me up: Lipps Diamond (guitar), Huggy Star (bass), and Sticks Dynamite (drums).

"Unfortunately, at this time cloning is not yet legal, but I am still experimenting in the lab."

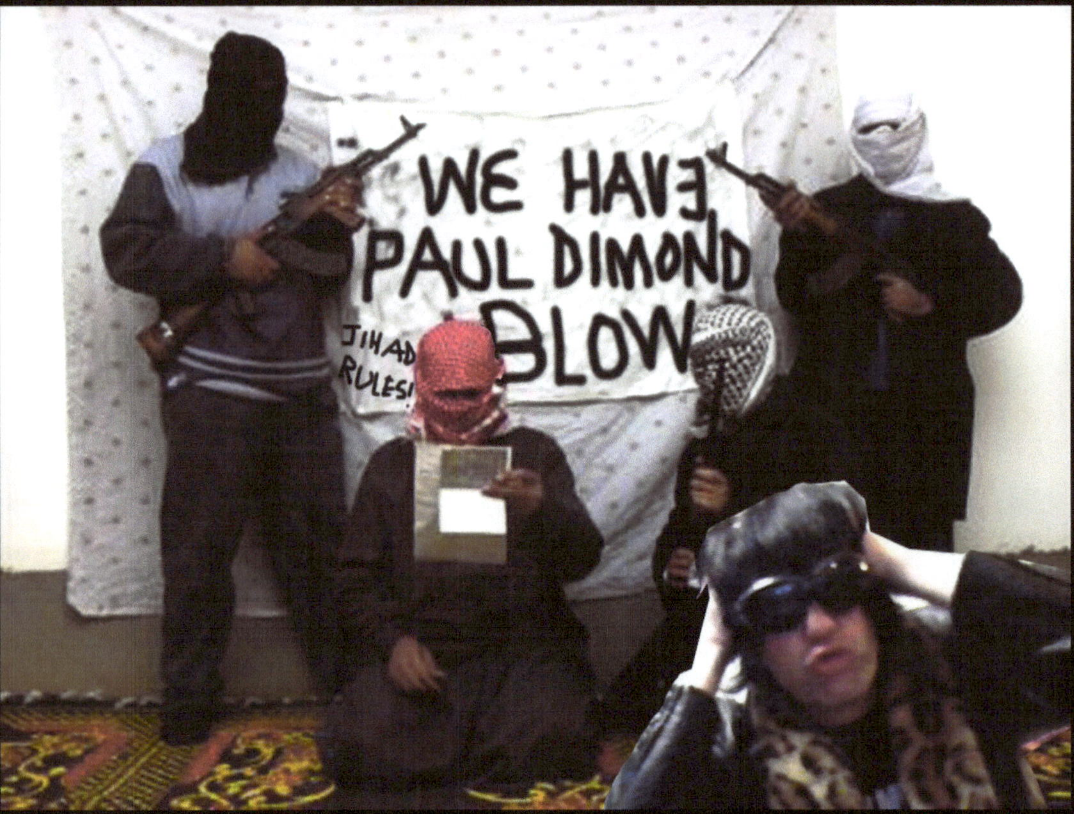

One time I was kidnapped by Myspace terrorists, who communicated their demands for my release via Myspace bulletins. No ransom was ever paid. Eventually, they let me go when the beer ran out. [Editor's note: you can read all about PDB's kidnapping in his book *Tales From Outer Space*]

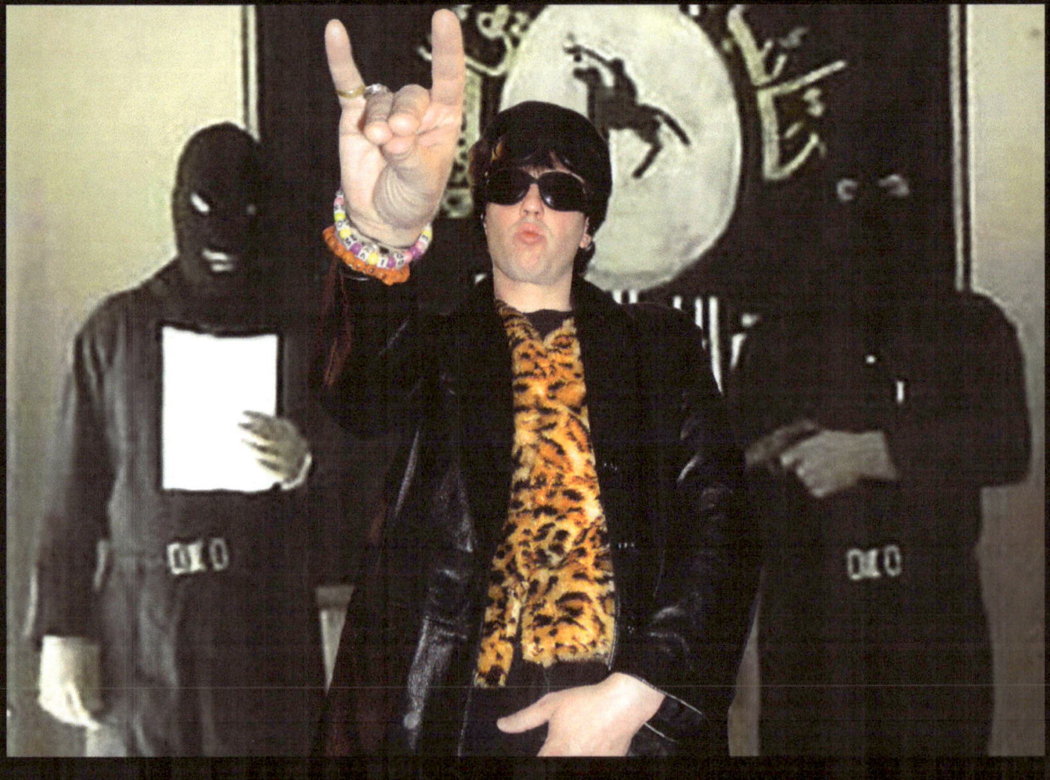

Back on Myspace, when it was still a popular social site, I introduced my new line of tighty whitey briefs... it almost got me banned for life... I often times embarrassed myself with photos such as this one (below), but they were always a hit with the ladies, who seemed to love them. And what's not to love, I ask you? They loved my profile pic, too.

"What's WHITE, TIGHT, and OUTASIGHT? My new line of PDB Tighty Whitey underwear... for men, women, and small animals."

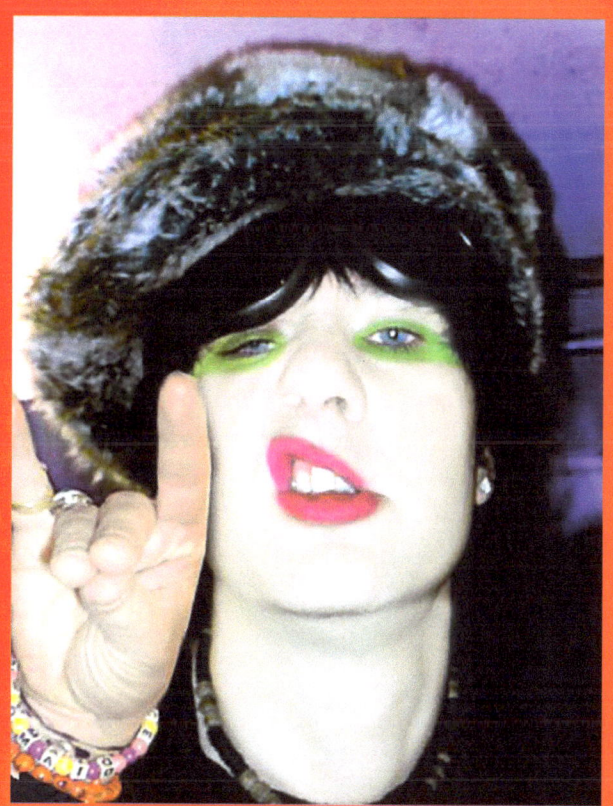

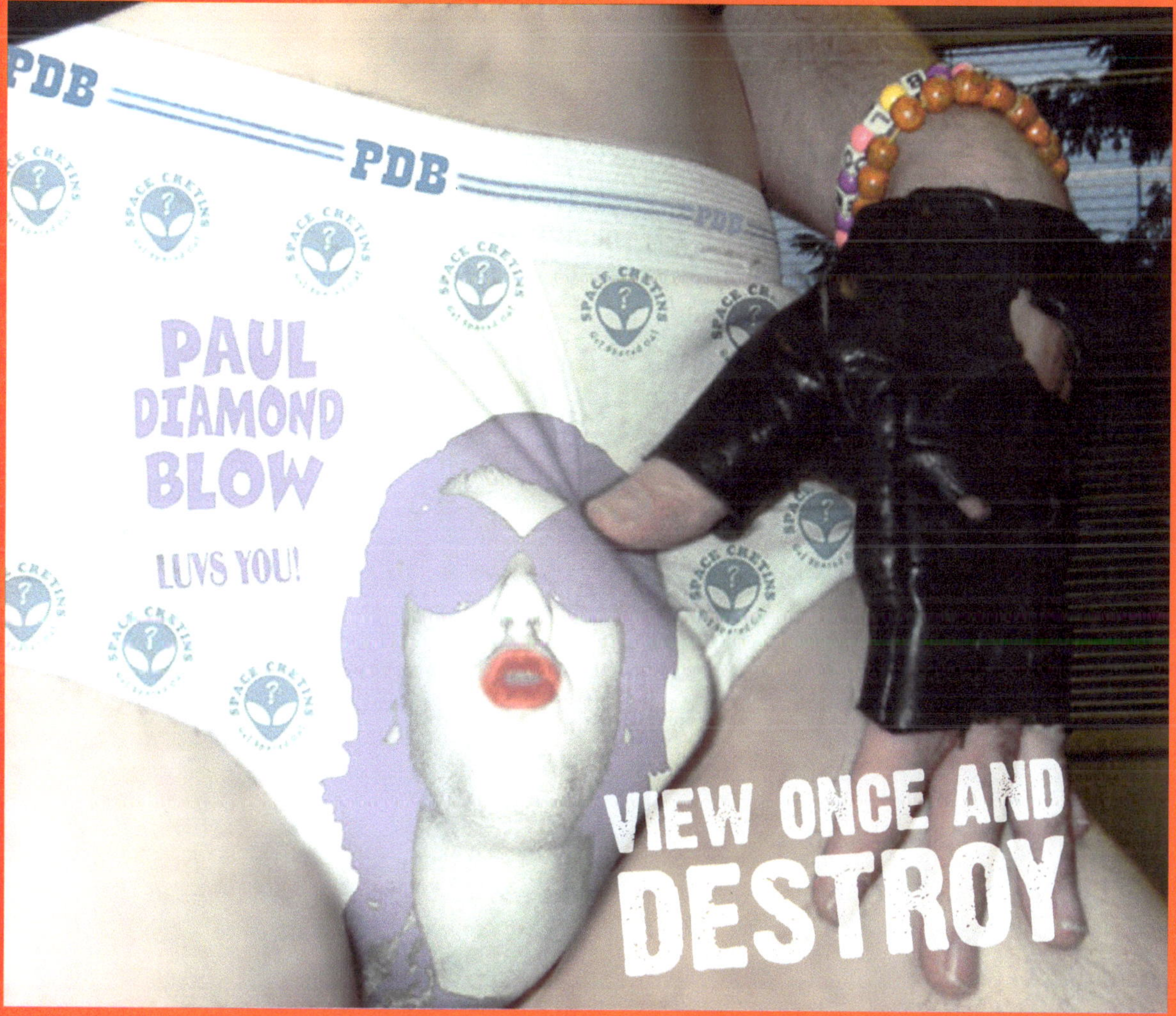

PDB PDB

SPACE CRETINS

PAUL DIAMOND BLOW

LUVS YOU!

VIEW ONCE AND DESTROY

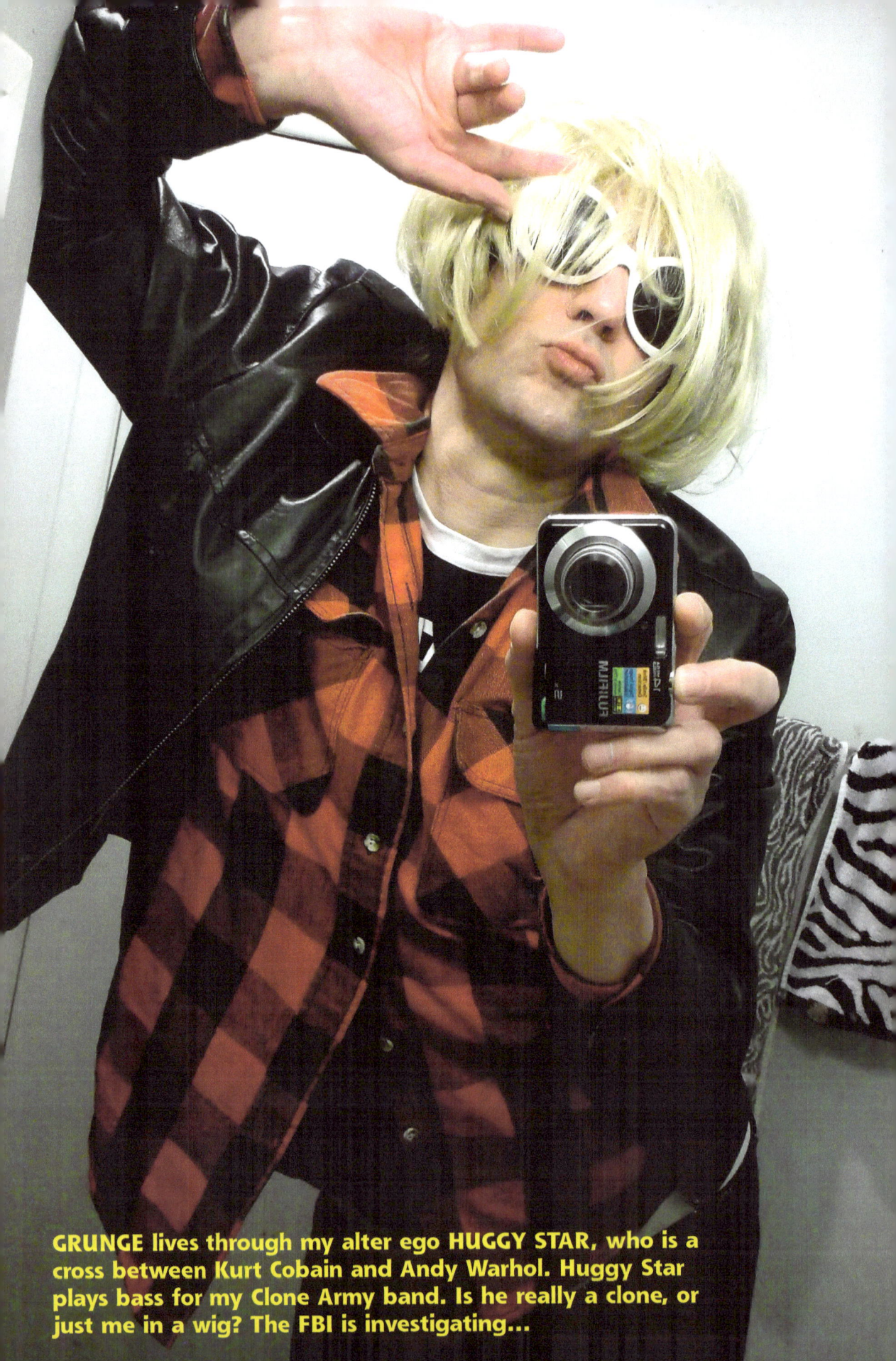

GRUNGE lives through my alter ego **HUGGY STAR**, who is a cross between Kurt Cobain and Andy Warhol. Huggy Star plays bass for my Clone Army band. Is he really a clone, or just me in a wig? The FBI is investigating…

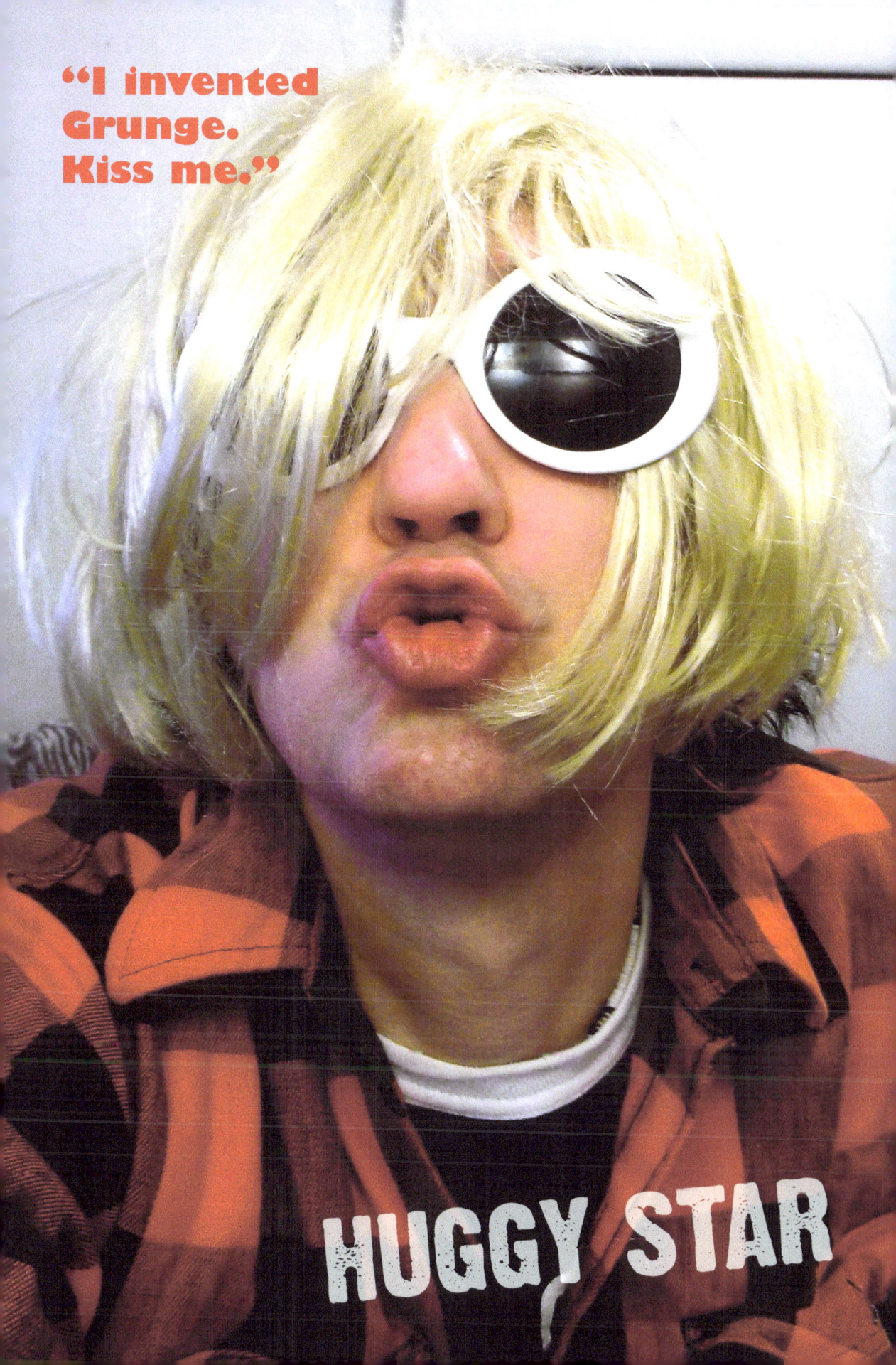

"I invented Grunge. Kiss me."

HUGGY STAR

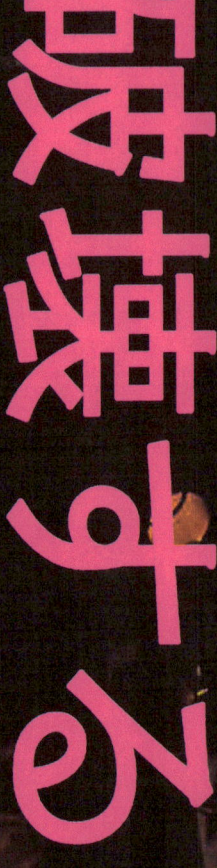

Performing at El Corazon, 2010

"Nothing says ROCK'N'ROLL like black leather and a white Les Paul!"

破壊する

Paul O Blon

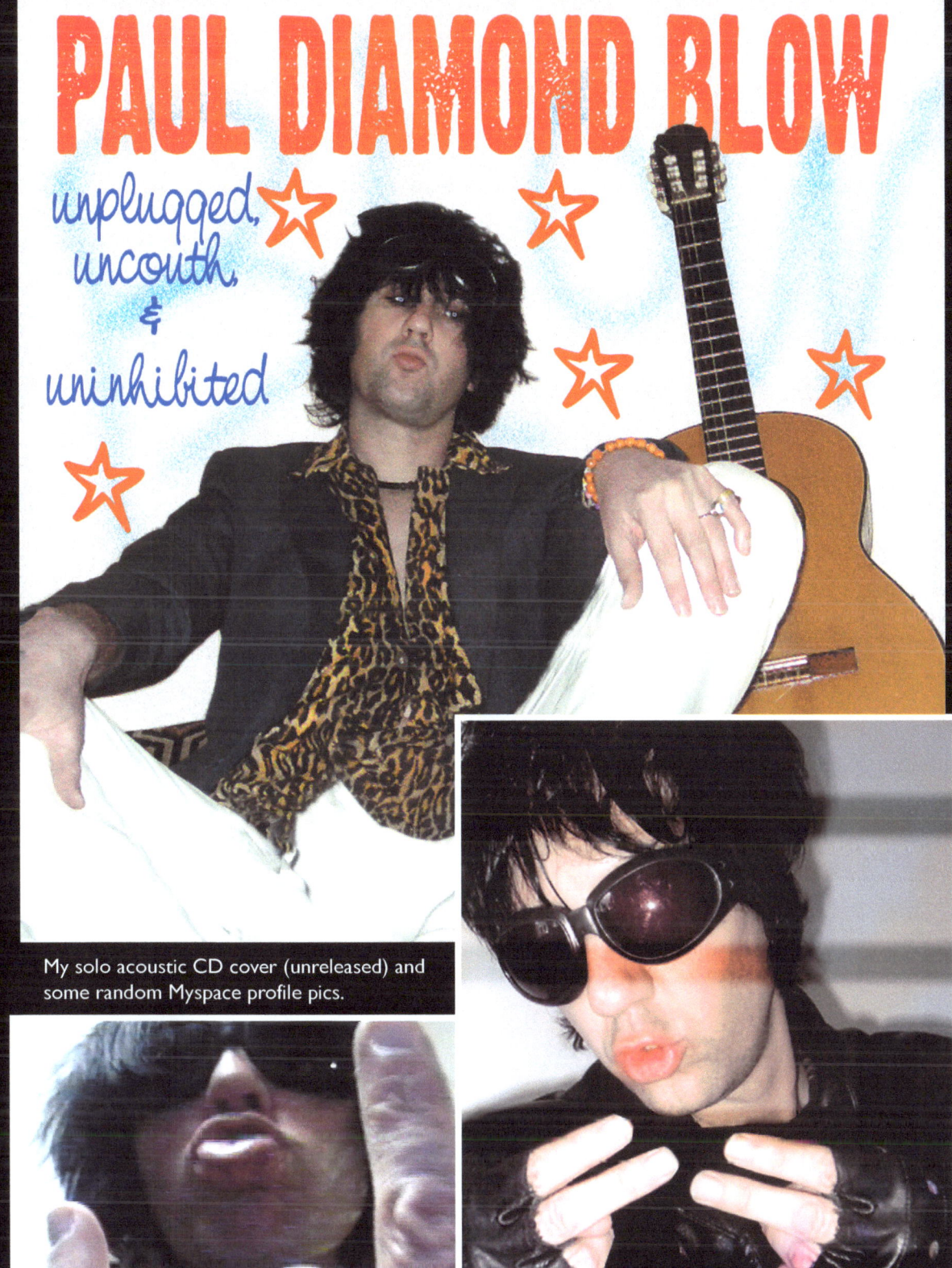

PAUL DIAMOND BLOW

unplugged, uncouth, & uninhibited

My solo acoustic CD cover (unreleased) and some random Myspace profile pics.

Starring PAUL DIAMOND BLOW as "Huggy Blow"

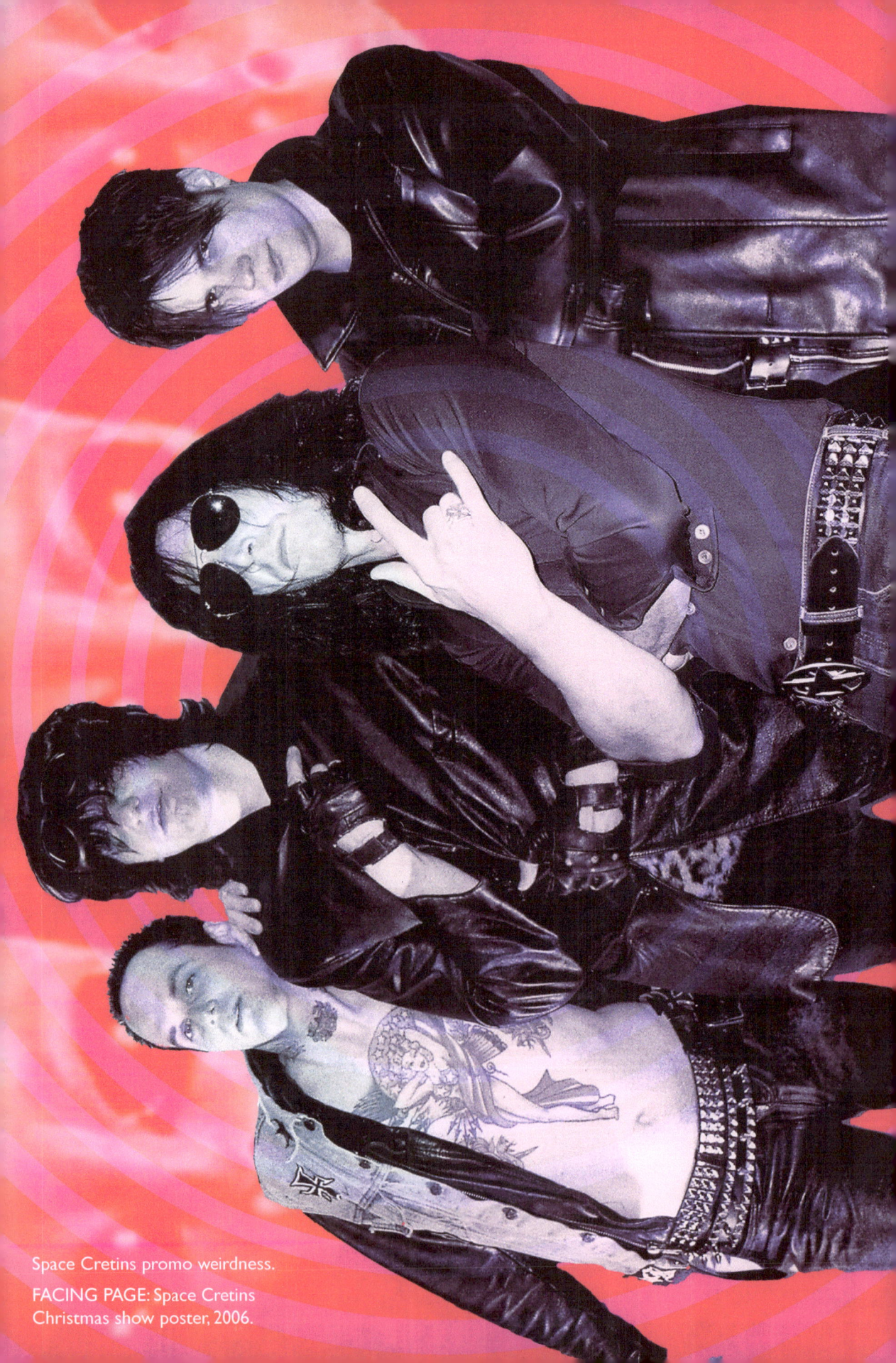

Space Cretins promo weirdness.

FACING PAGE: Space Cretins
Christmas show poster, 2006.

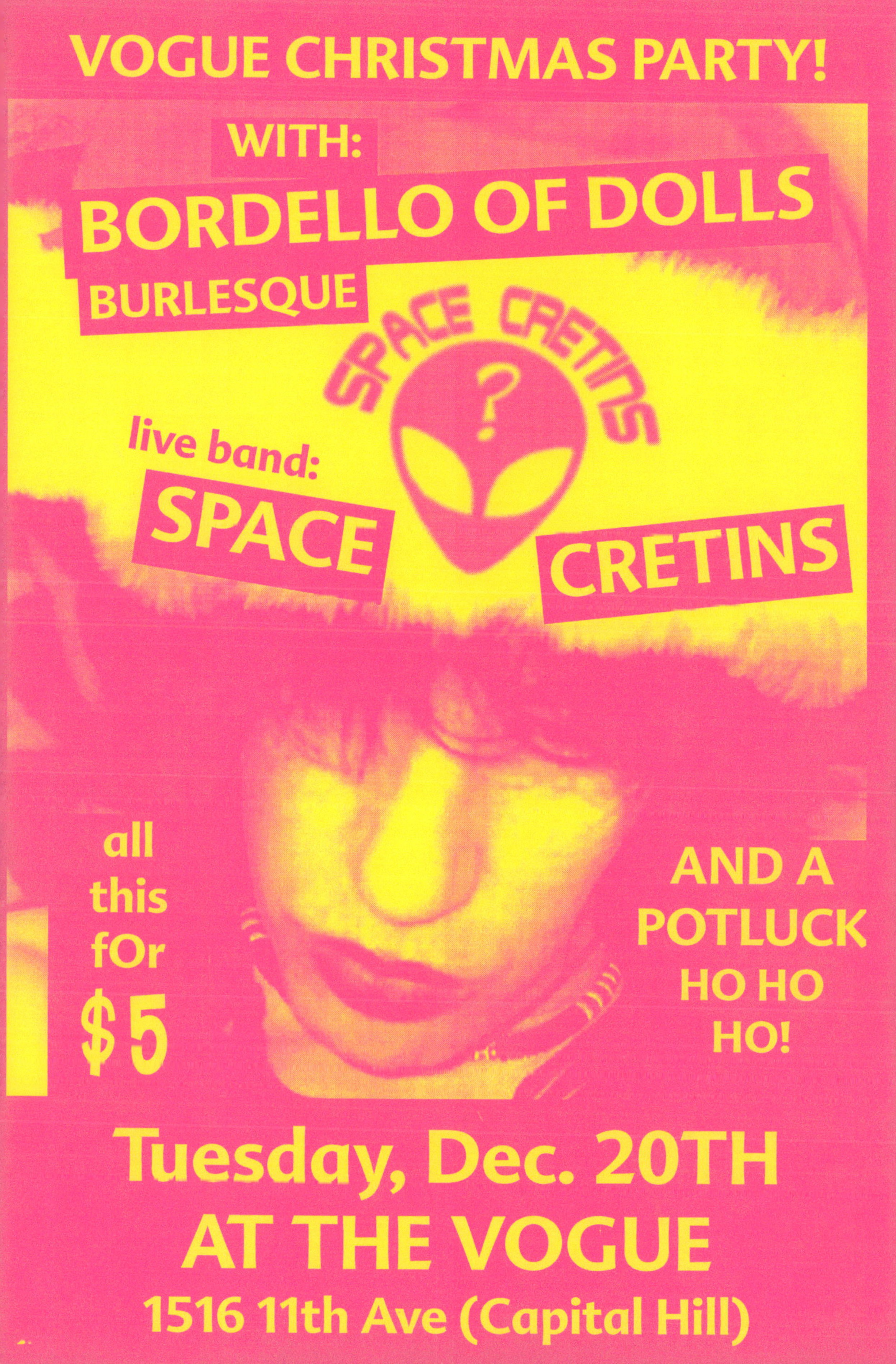

VOGUE CHRISTMAS PARTY!

WITH:

BORDELLO OF DOLLS
BURLESQUE

live band:
SPACE   CRETINS

SPACE CRETINS ?

all this fOr $5

AND A POTLUCK
HO HO HO!

Tuesday, Dec. 20TH
AT THE VOGUE
1516 11th Ave (Capital Hill)

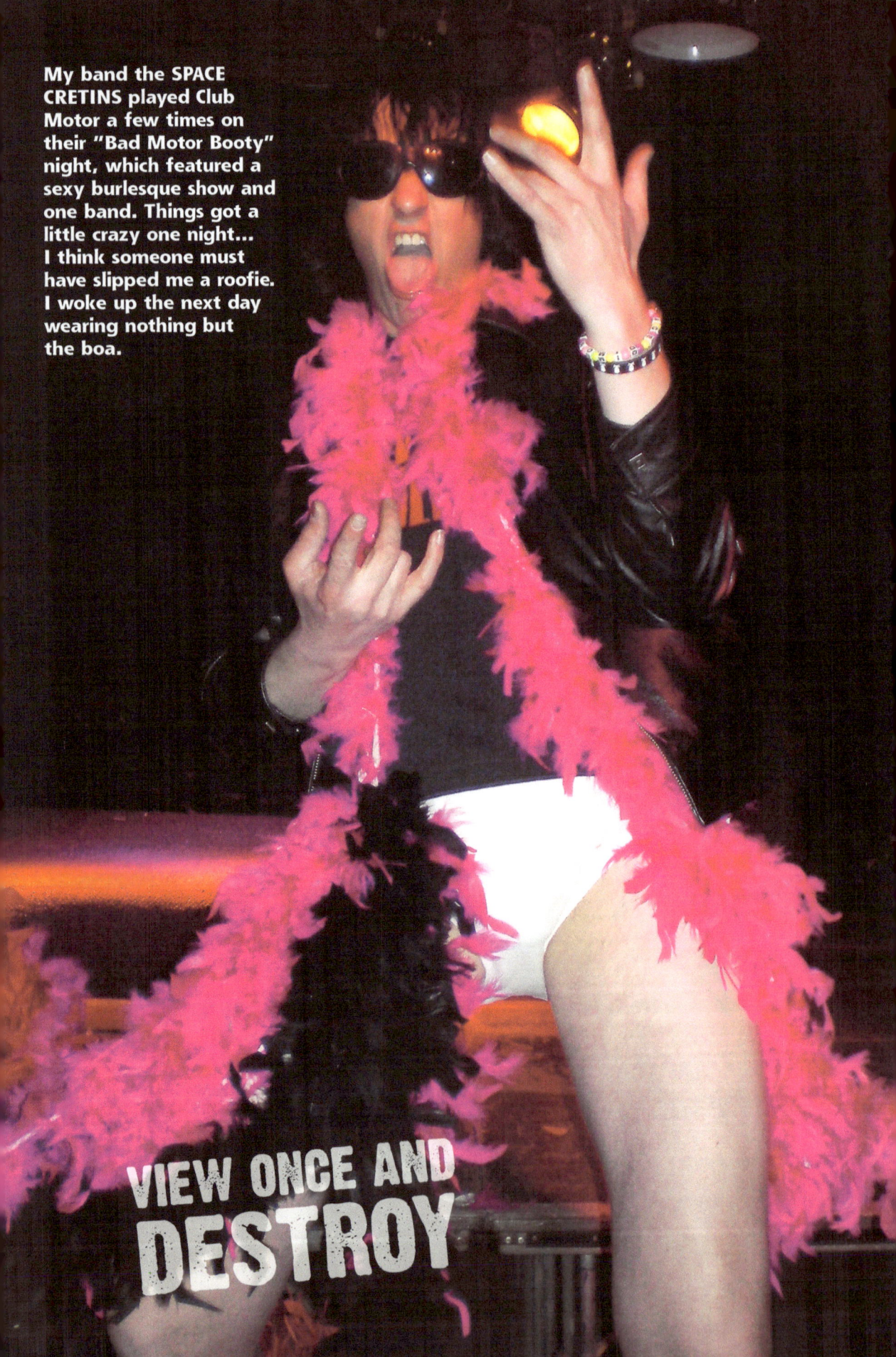

My band the SPACE CRETINS played Club Motor a few times on their "Bad Motor Booty" night, which featured a sexy burlesque show and one band. Things got a little crazy one night... I think someone must have slipped me a roofie. I woke up the next day wearing nothing but the boa.

VIEW ONCE AND
DESTROY

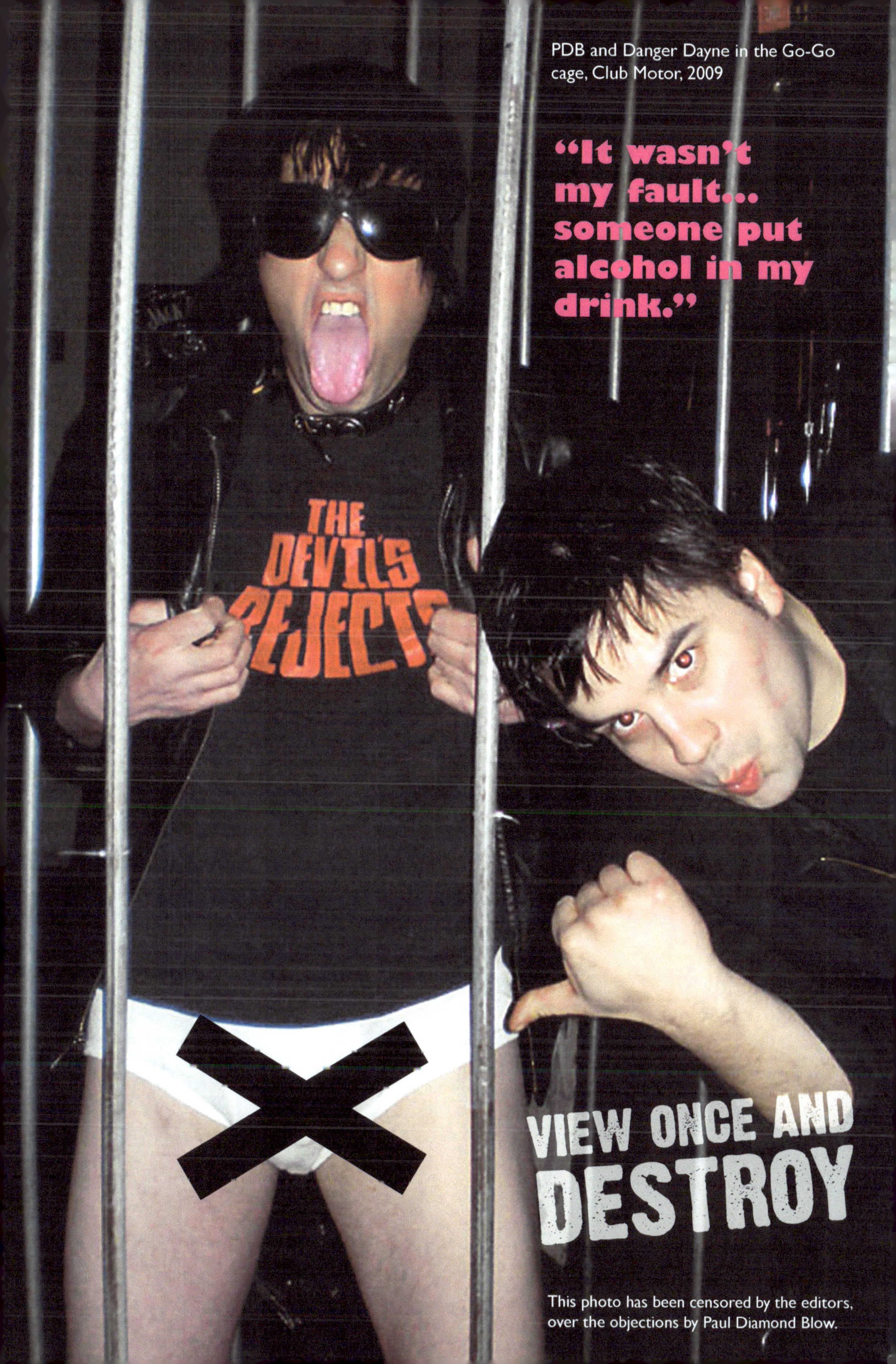

PDB and Danger Dayne in the Go-Go cage, Club Motor, 2009

"It wasn't my fault... someone put alcohol in my drink."

VIEW ONCE AND DESTROY

This photo has been censored by the editors, over the objections by Paul Diamond Blow.

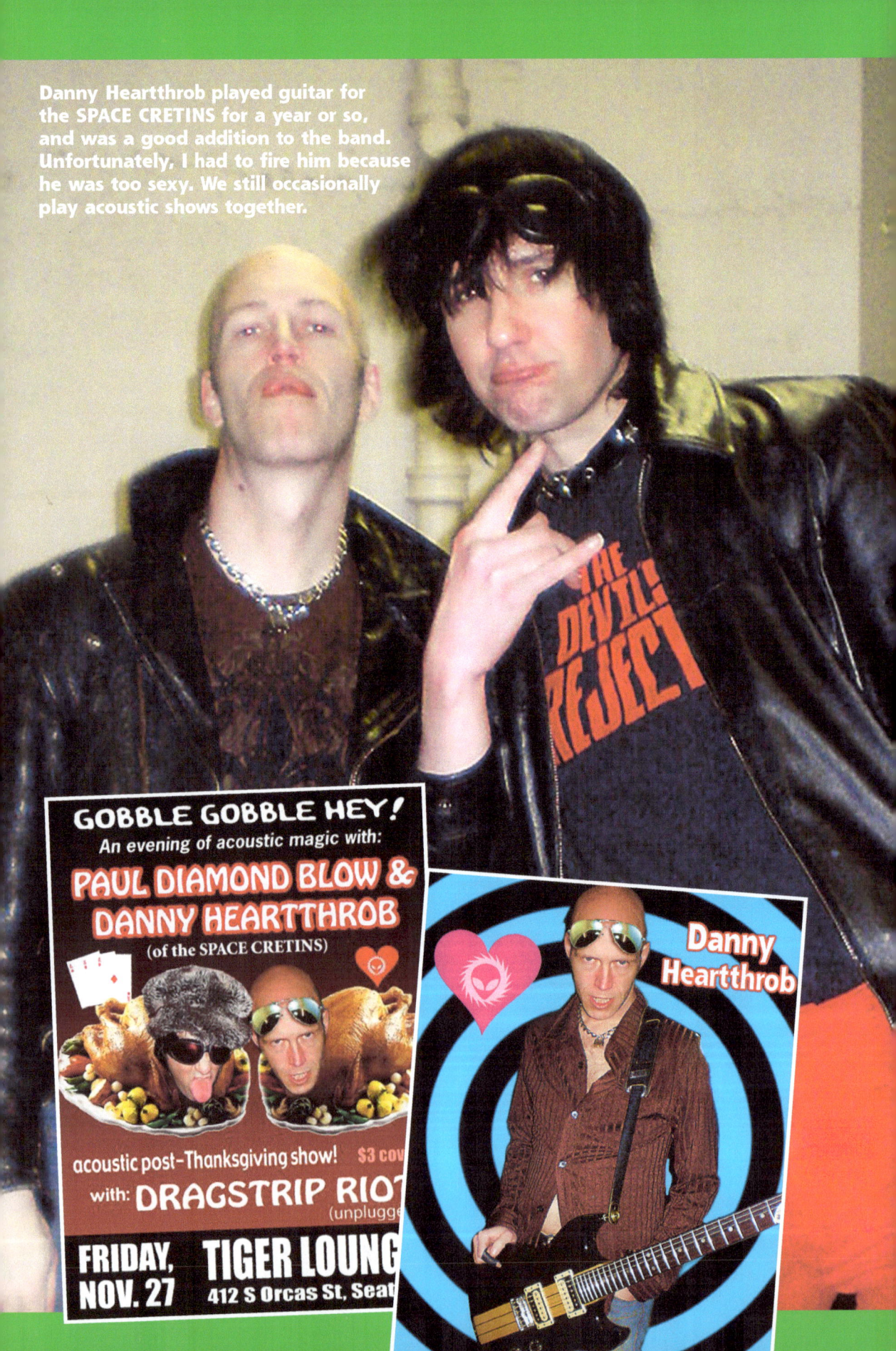

Danny Heartthrob played guitar for the SPACE CRETINS for a year or so, and was a good addition to the band. Unfortunately, I had to fire him because he was too sexy. We still occasionally play acoustic shows together.

GOBBLE GOBBLE HEY!

An evening of acoustic magic with:

PAUL DIAMOND BLOW & DANNY HEARTTHROB
(of the SPACE CRETINS)

acoustic post-Thanksgiving show! $3 cov

with: DRAGSTRIP RIOT
(unplugge

FRIDAY, NOV. 27   TIGER LOUNG
412 S Orcas St, Seat

Danny Heartthrob

"I have been known to pout on stage if I don't get my drink tickets in a timely manner..."

PDB at Club Motor, 2009

VIEW ONCE AND DESTROY

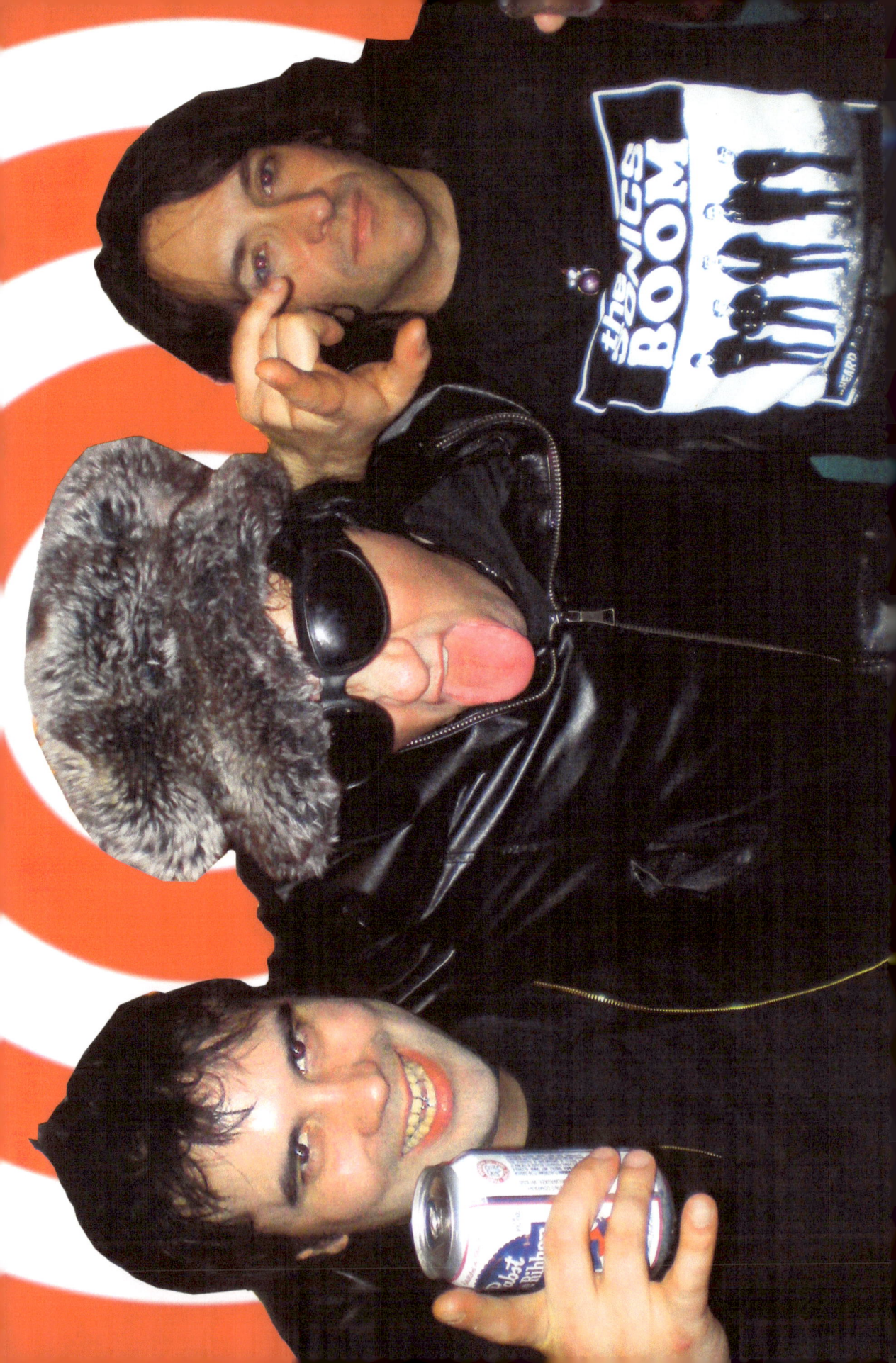

The Funhouse was the coolest punk rock dive bar/club in Seattle during the decade of 2000-2010. My bands played there many times, and it was always a lot of fun. I had a lot of good times in the Funhouse backstage room. Here I am backstage with SPACE CRETINS members Danger Dayne and Scotty Astronaughty. What happens in the backstage room, stays in the backstage room. Had a lot of good times in the Funhouse backstage bathroom, too.

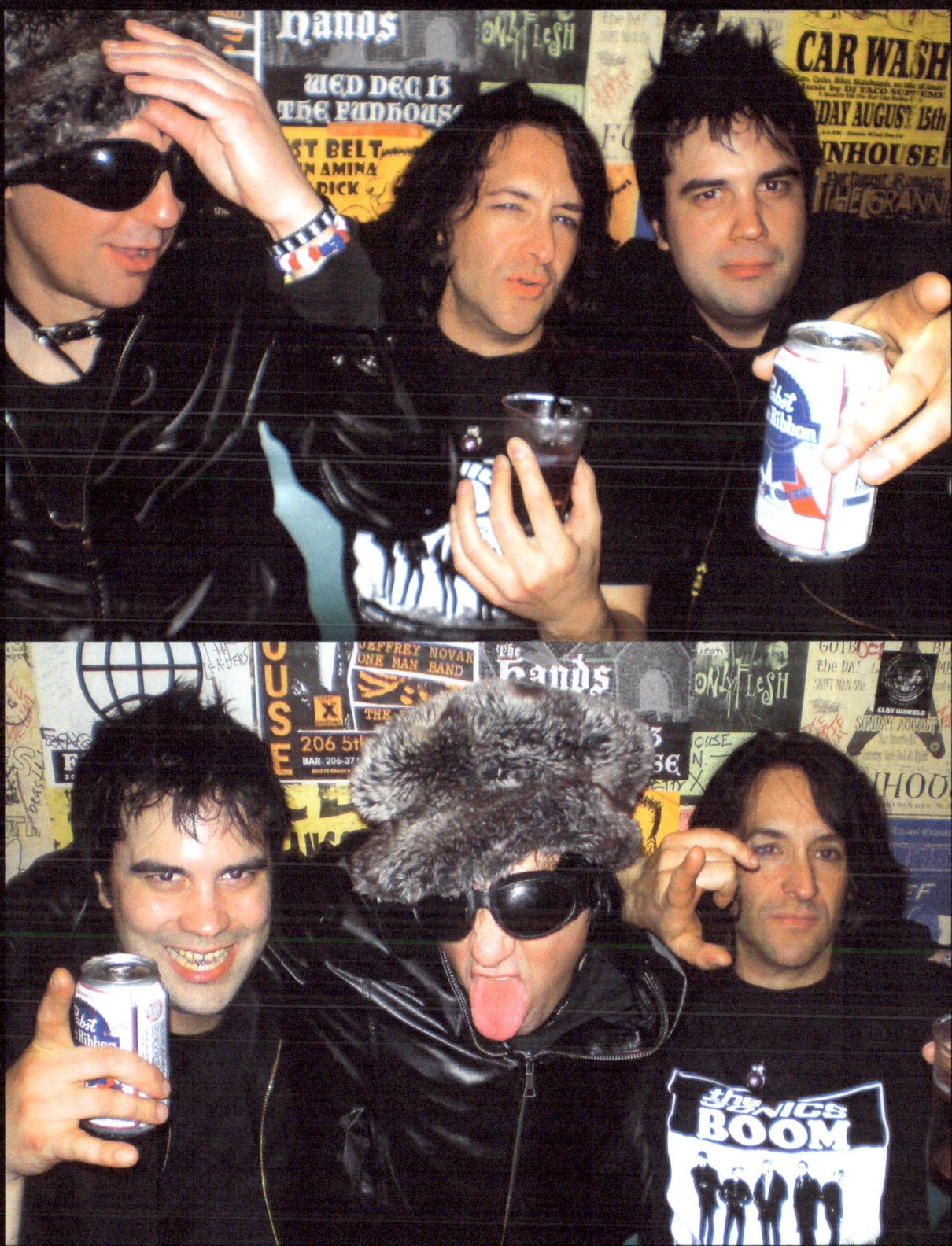

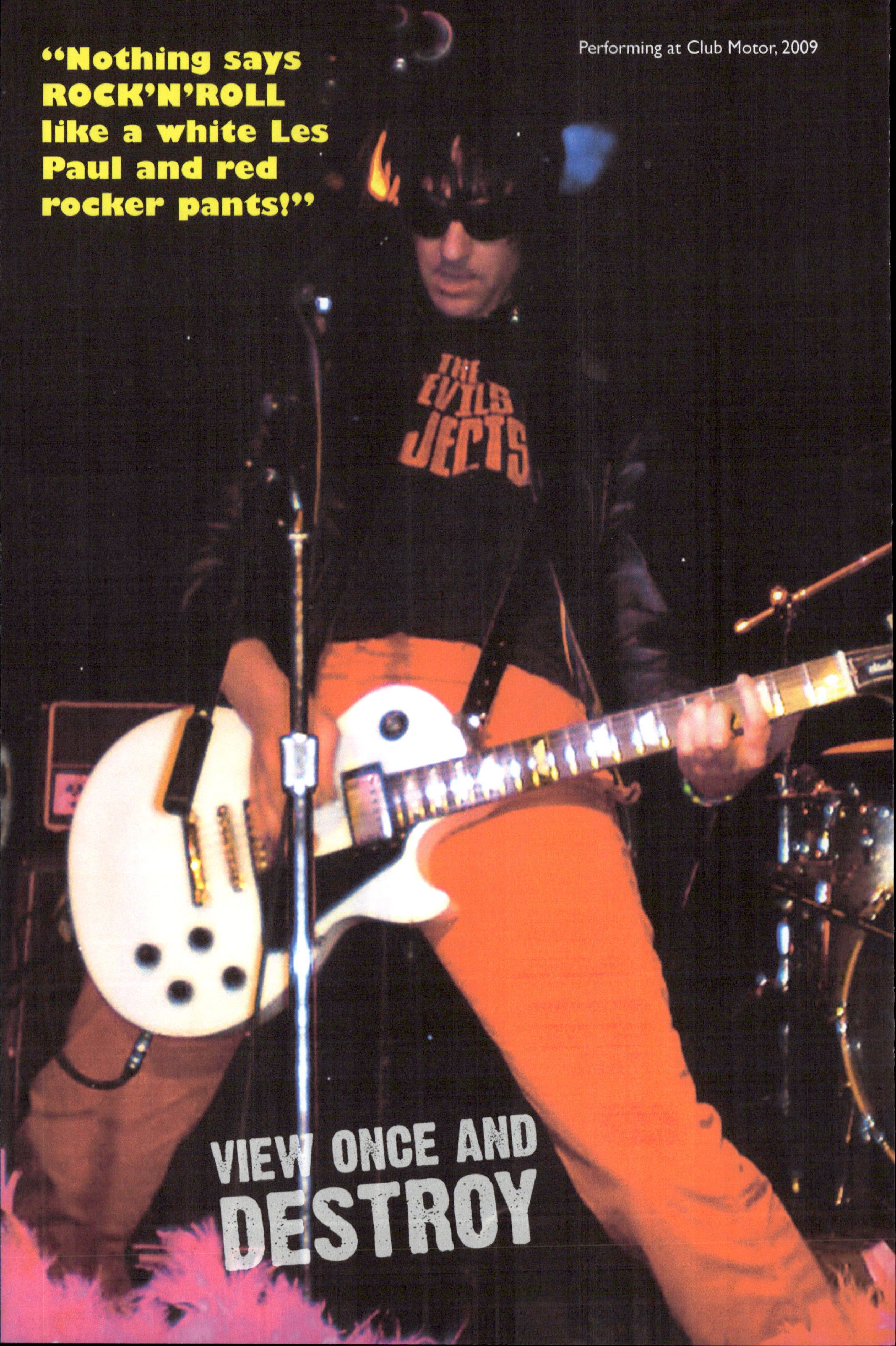

"Nothing says ROCK'N'ROLL like a white Les Paul and red rocker pants!"

VIEW ONCE AND DESTROY

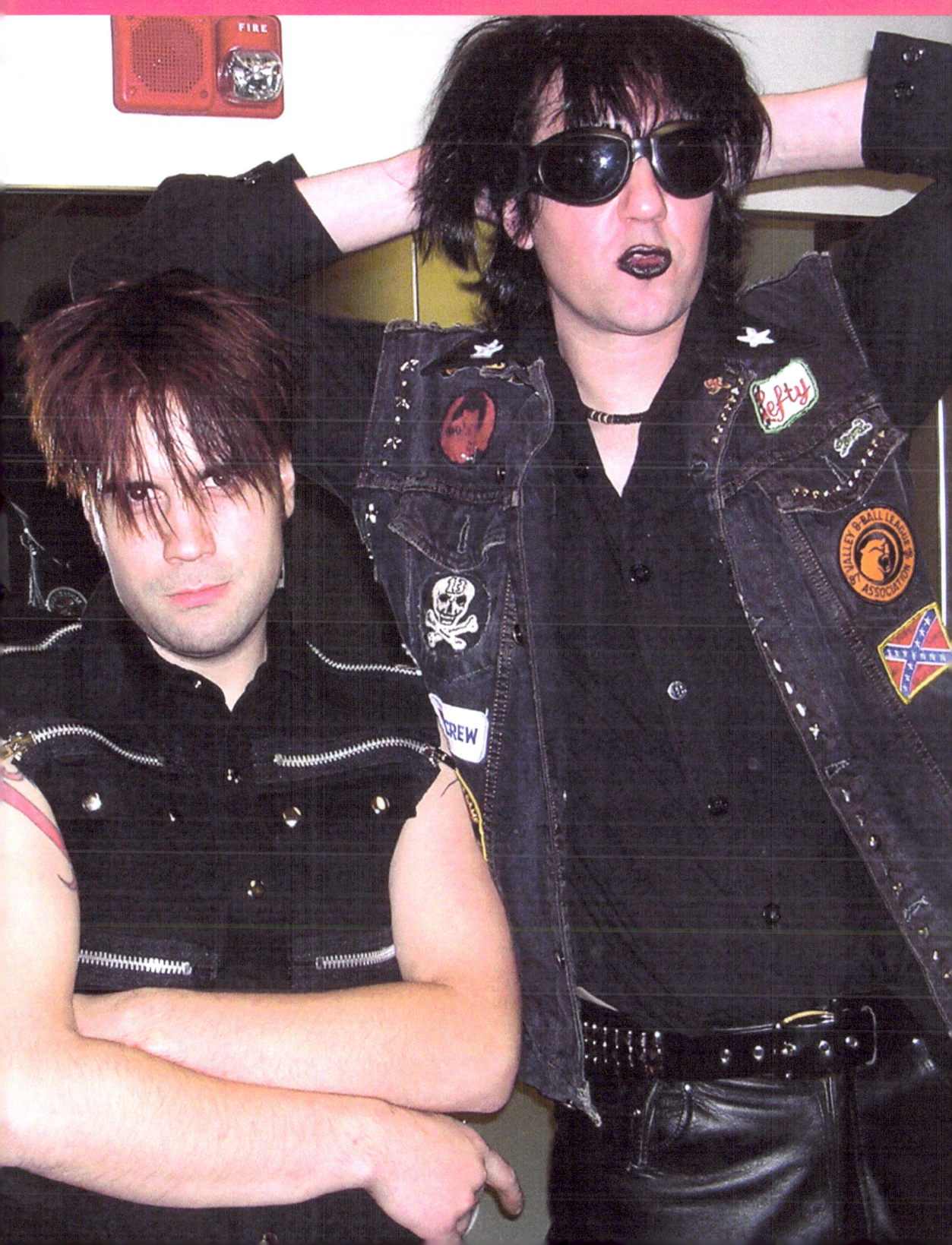

Danger Dayne and I have been rocking together in bands for a long time now. He's an awesome drummer and a sweetheart of a guy. He first joined my band when I won him in a poker game. Here we are hanging out in the ladies bathroom at the Premier, before a SPACE CRETINS gig. Don't even ASK what we were doing in the ladies room...

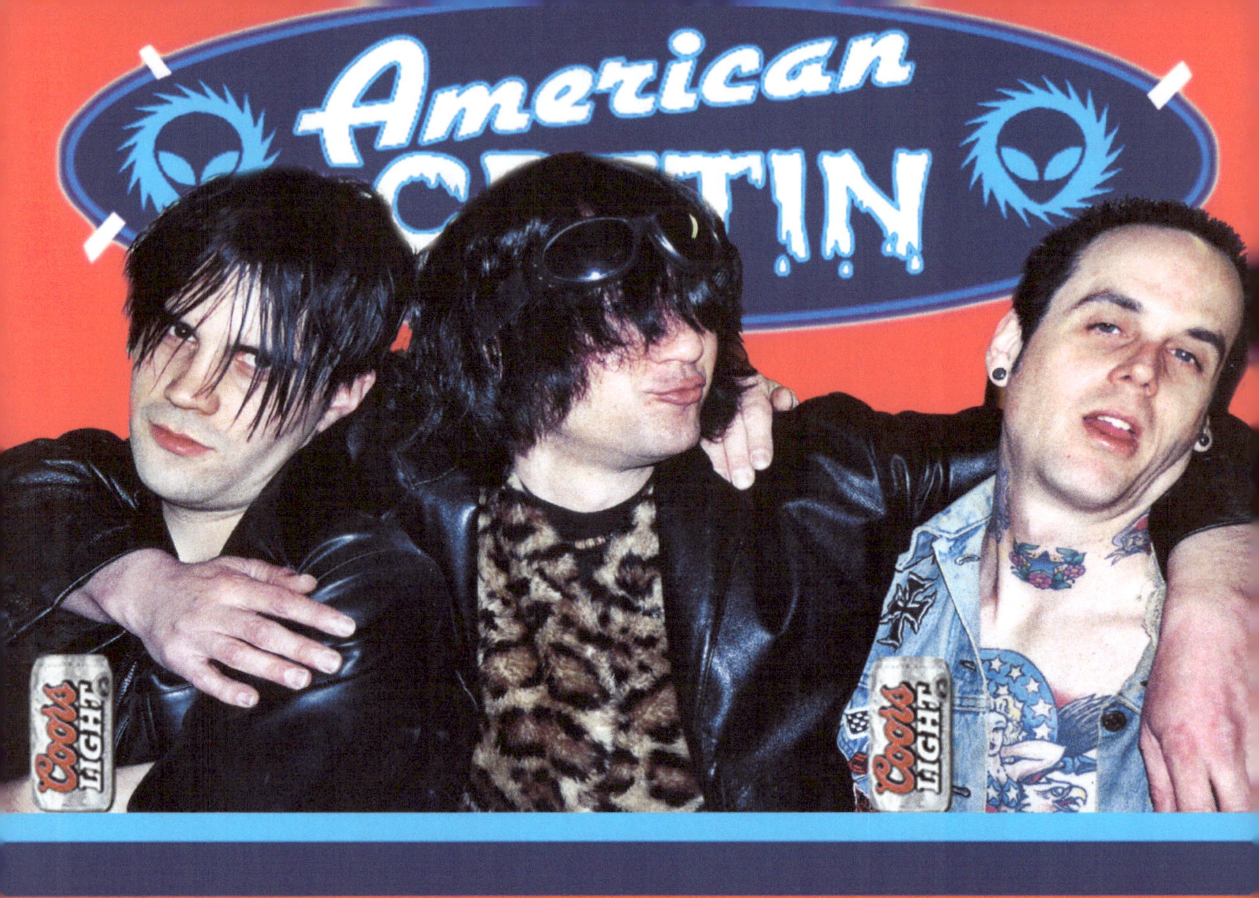

The **SPACE CRETINS** had a TV show broadcast on Seattle's public access cable station, one episode every season. The episode that featured the animated cartoon was a smash hit. In 2012 we even made a comic book to promote a reunion gig... reproduced here in full on the following pages, complete with bonus "epilogue" pages that were not included in the actual comic book.

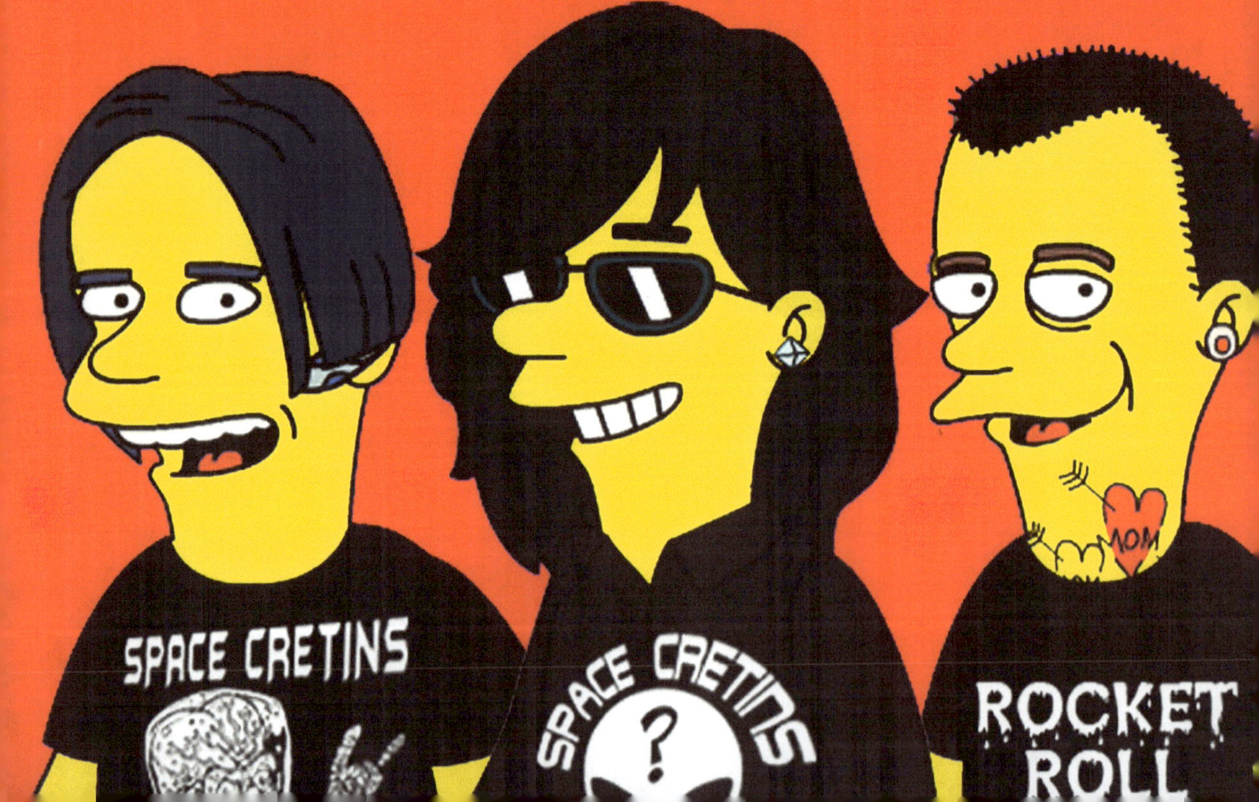

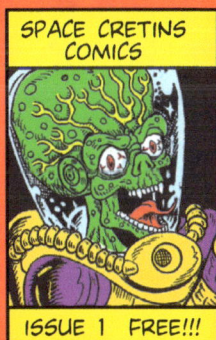

SPACE 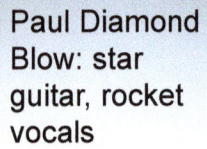 CRETINS

CAST OF CHARACTERS:

Paul Diamond Blow: star guitar, rocket vocals

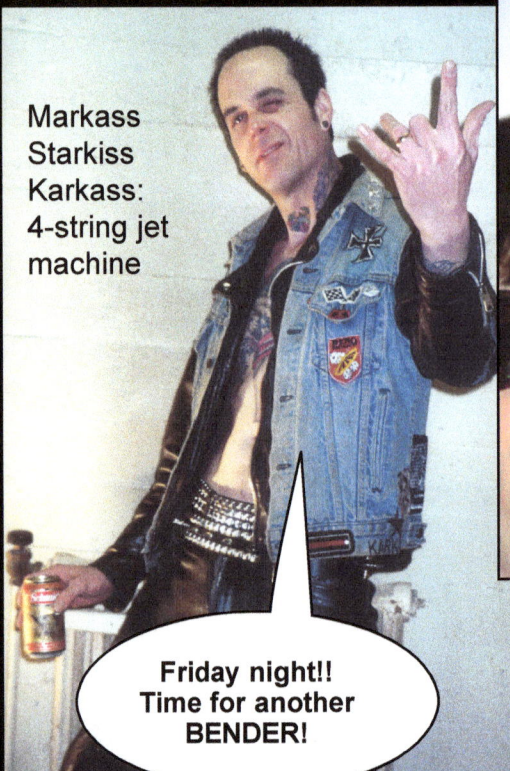

Markass Starkiss Karkass: 4-string jet machine

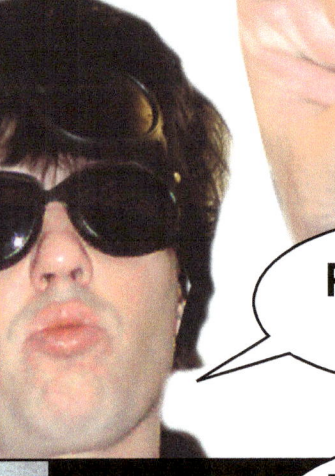

PARTY ON, DUDES!!!

Friday night!! Time for another BENDER!

THIS IS INSANE... *INSANE* I TELL YOU!!!

Danger Dayne: Drum Commander

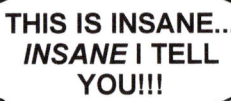

William Shatner: manager and spiritual advisor

Gentlemen, I propose we boldly go on a *five-year* tour!

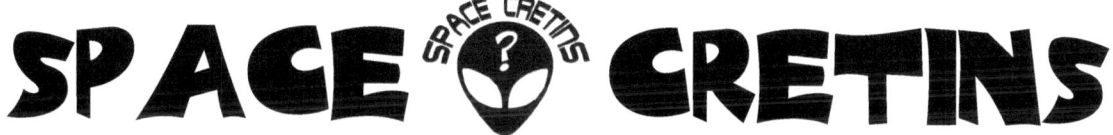

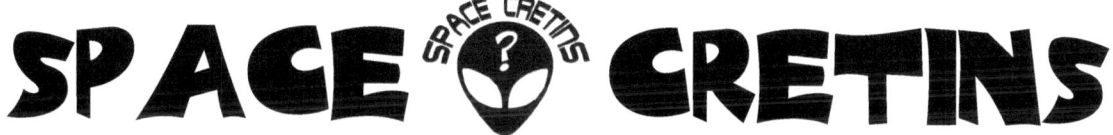

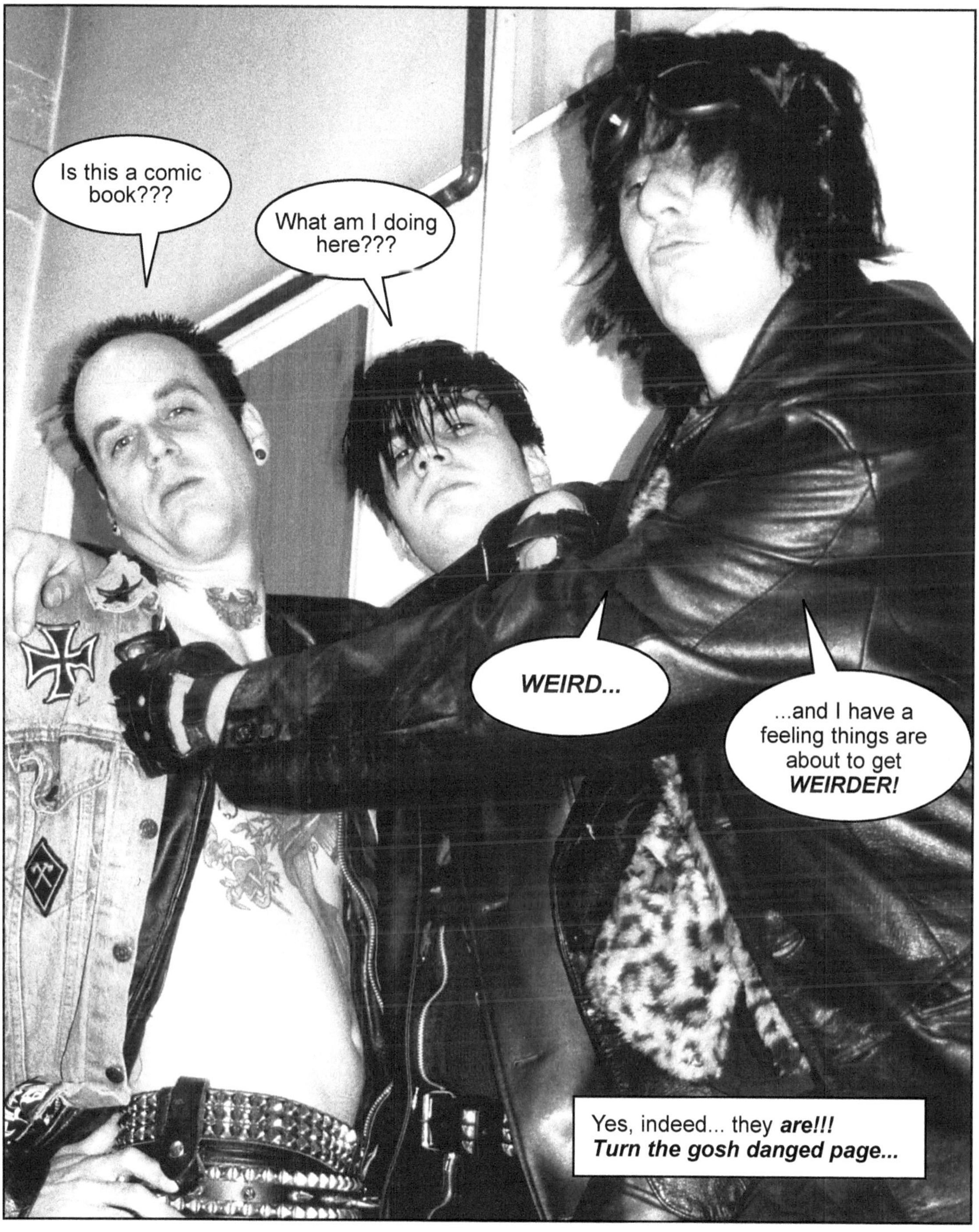

The year: 2004. Another sold out SPACE CRETINS show at the Sunset Tavern.

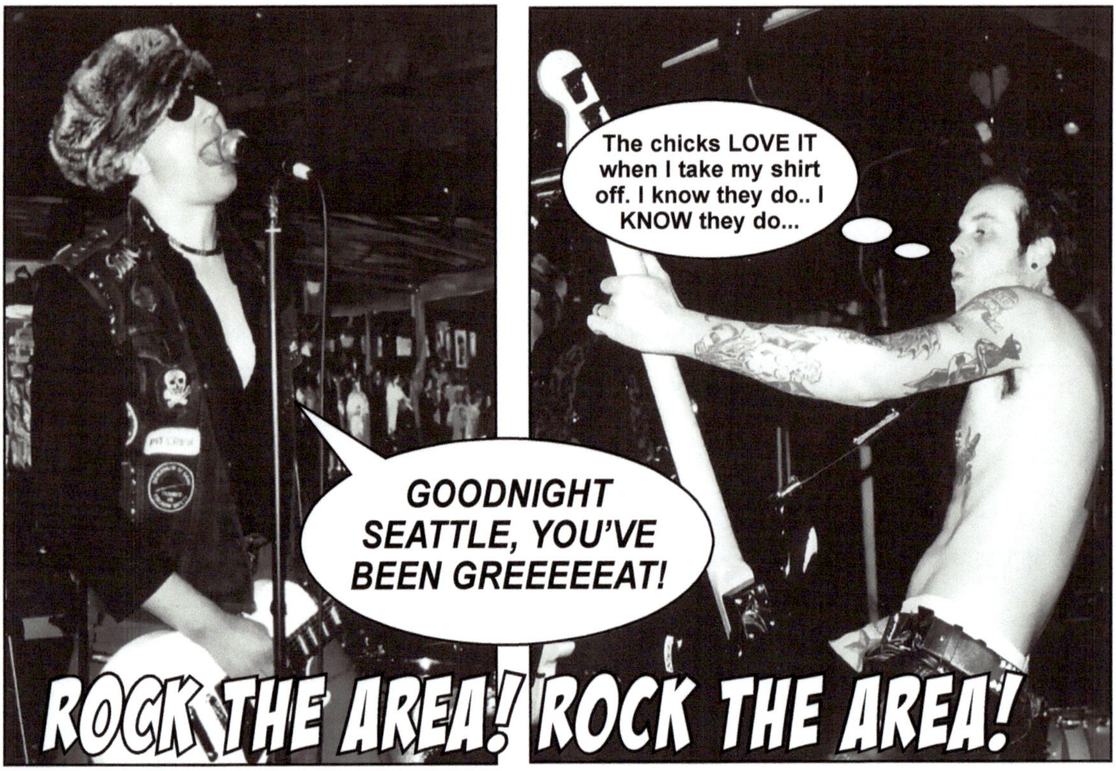

The chicks LOVE IT when I take my shirt off. I know they do.. I KNOW they do...

GOODNIGHT SEATTLE, YOU'VE BEEN GREEEEEAT!

ROCK THE AREA! ROCK THE AREA!

Later, backstage... The band unwinds and plans the next step toward WORLD DOMINATION...

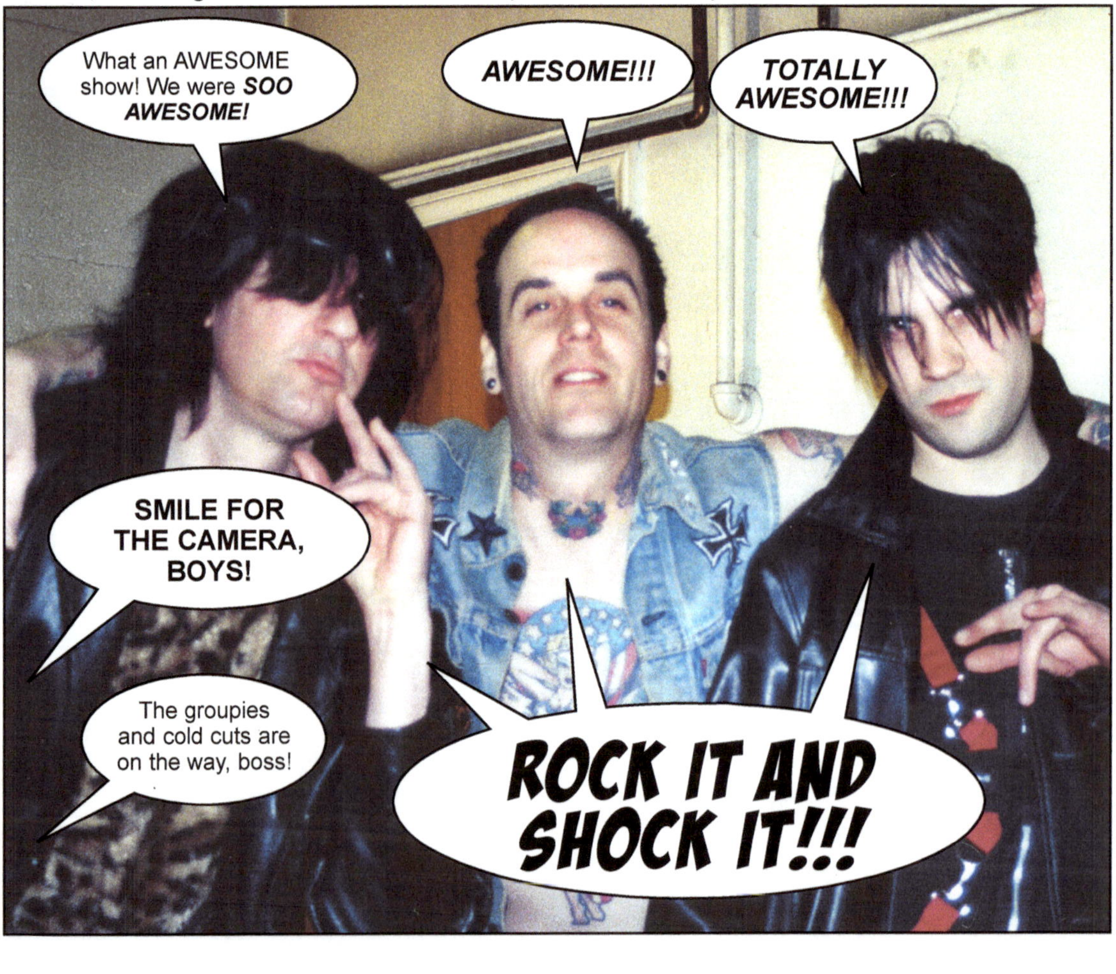

What an AWESOME show! We were SOO AWESOME!

AWESOME!!!

TOTALLY AWESOME!!!

SMILE FOR THE CAMERA, BOYS!

The groupies and cold cuts are on the way, boss!

ROCK IT AND SHOCK IT!!!

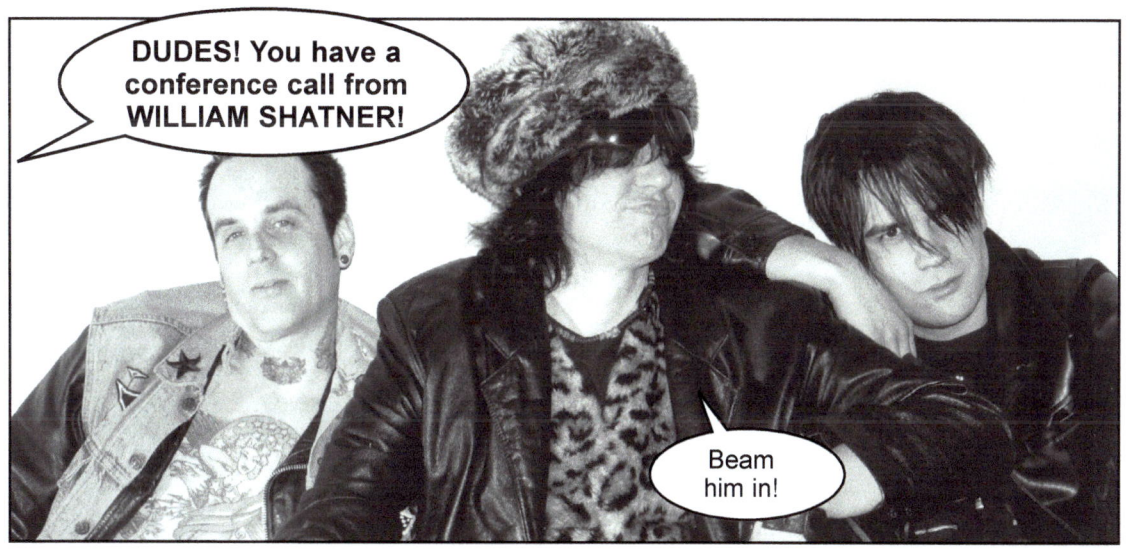

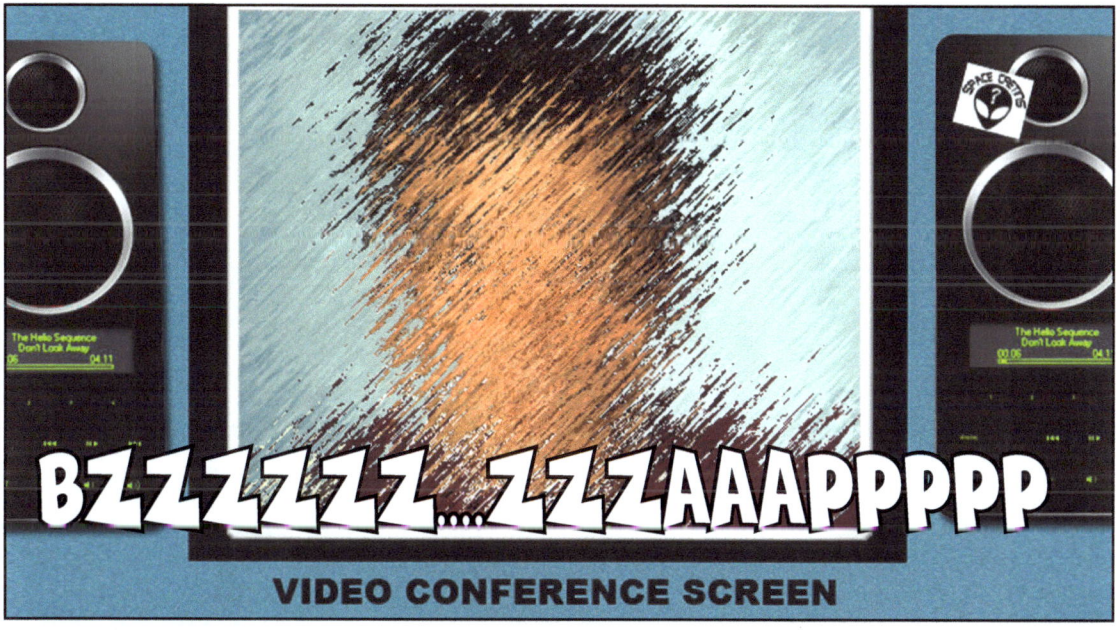

VIDEO CONFERENCE SCREEN

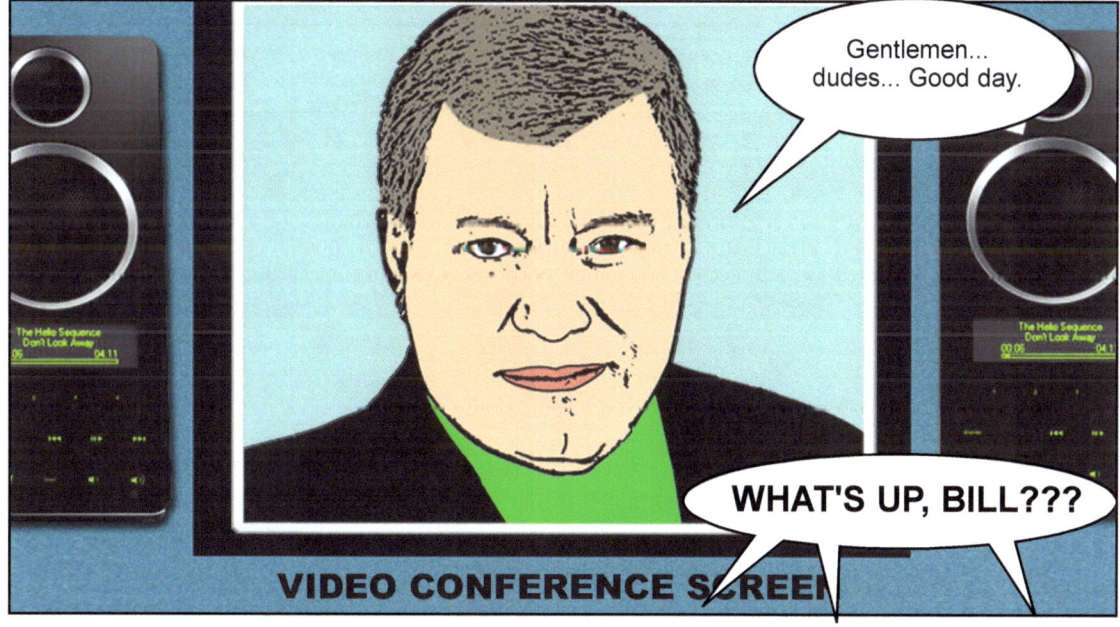

VIDEO CONFERENCE SCREEN

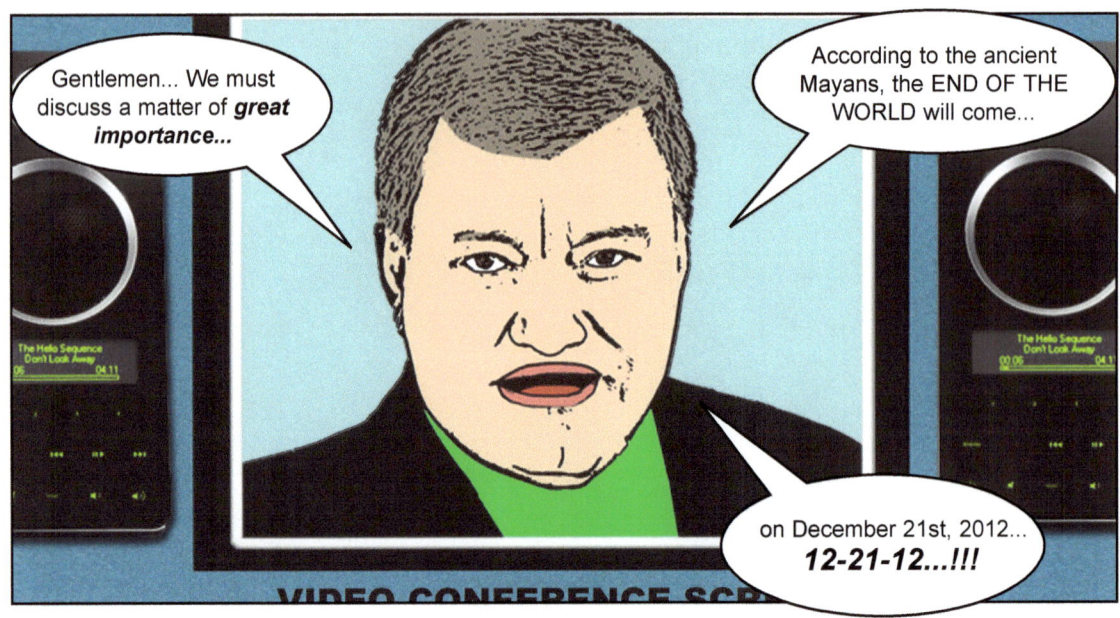

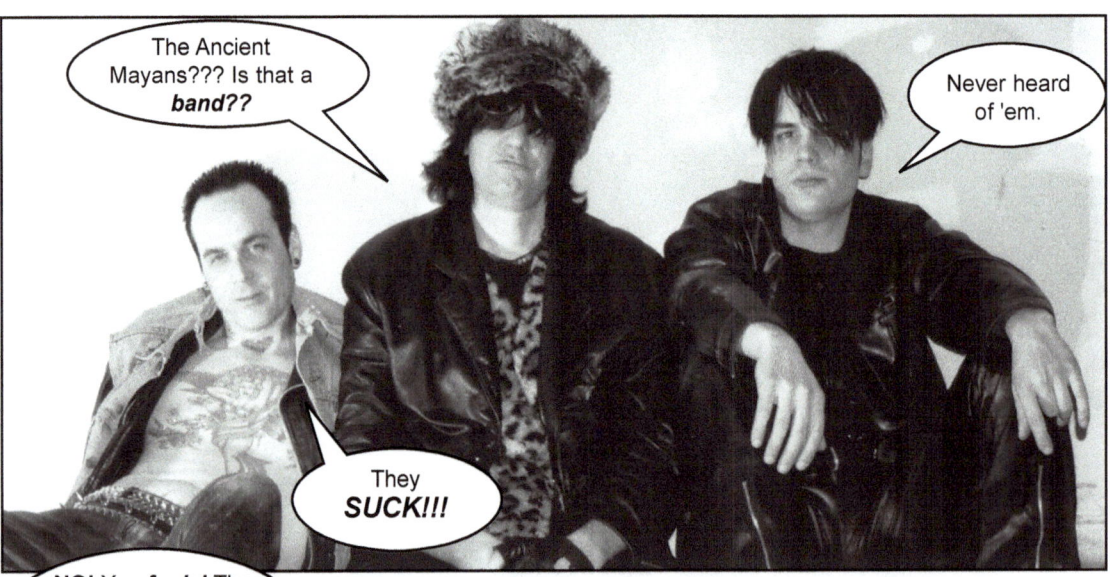

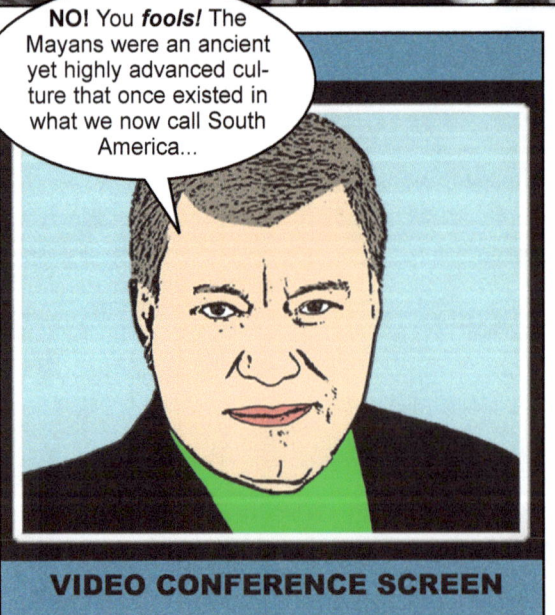

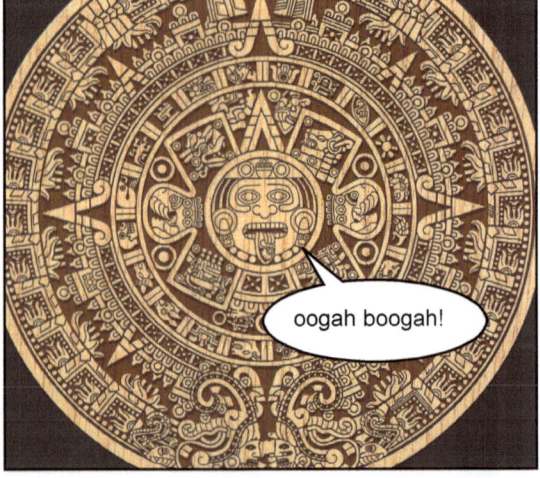

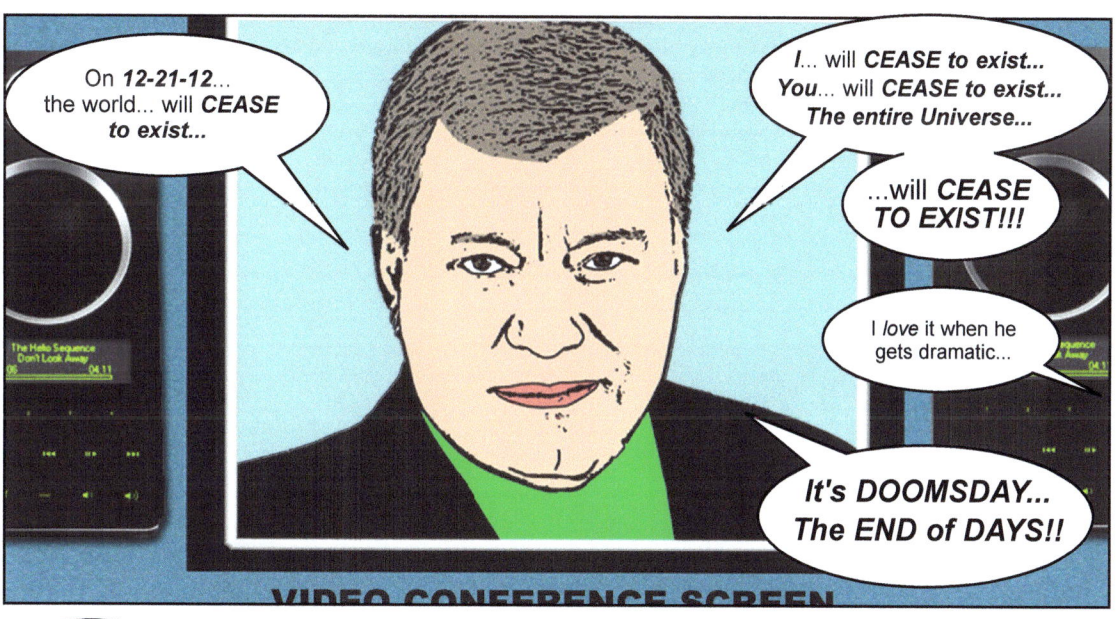

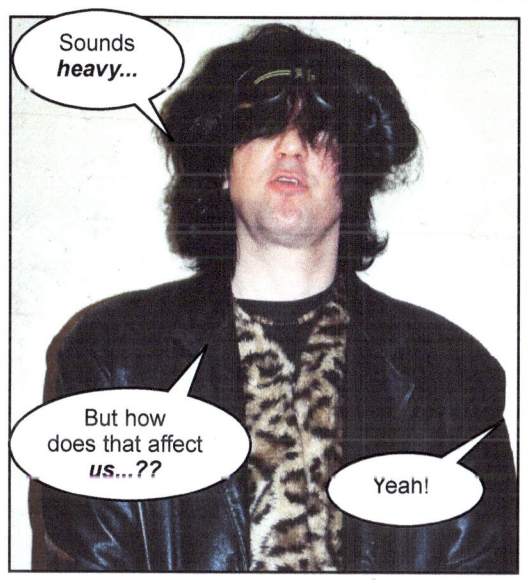

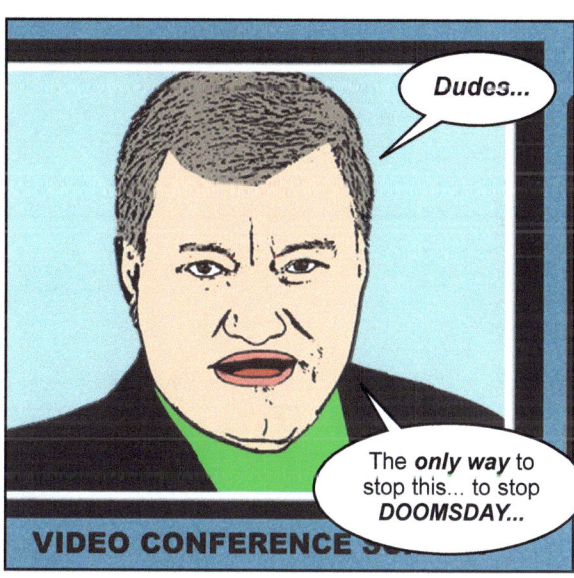

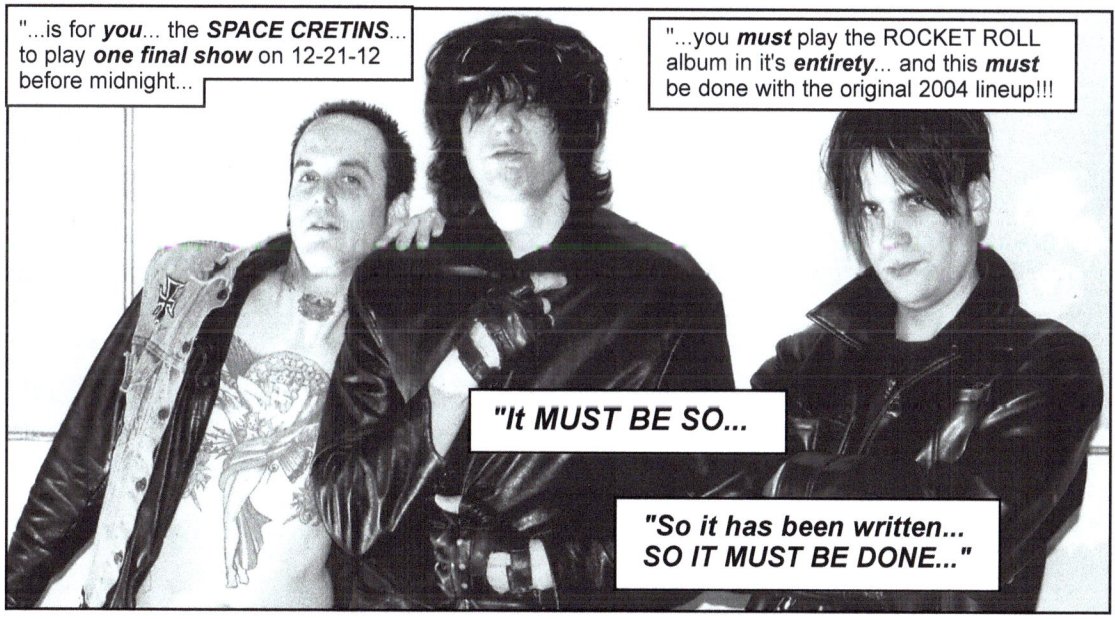

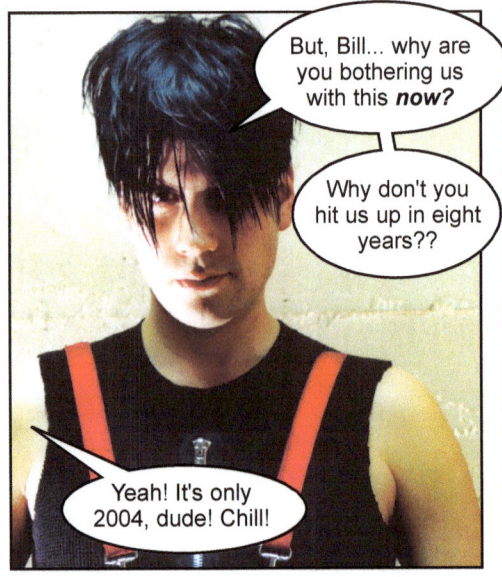

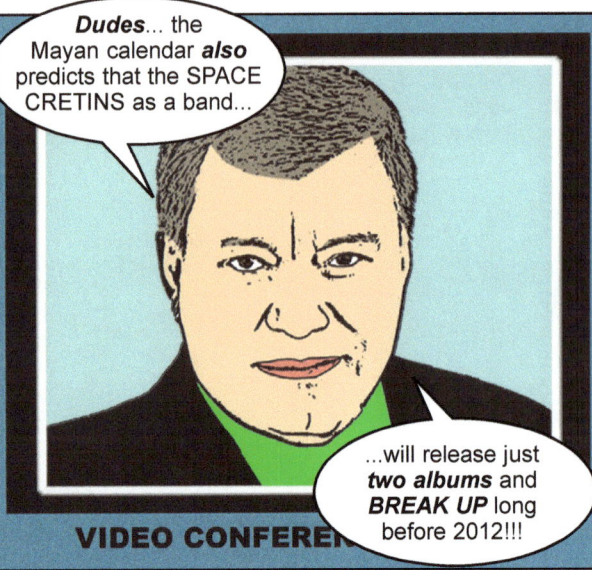

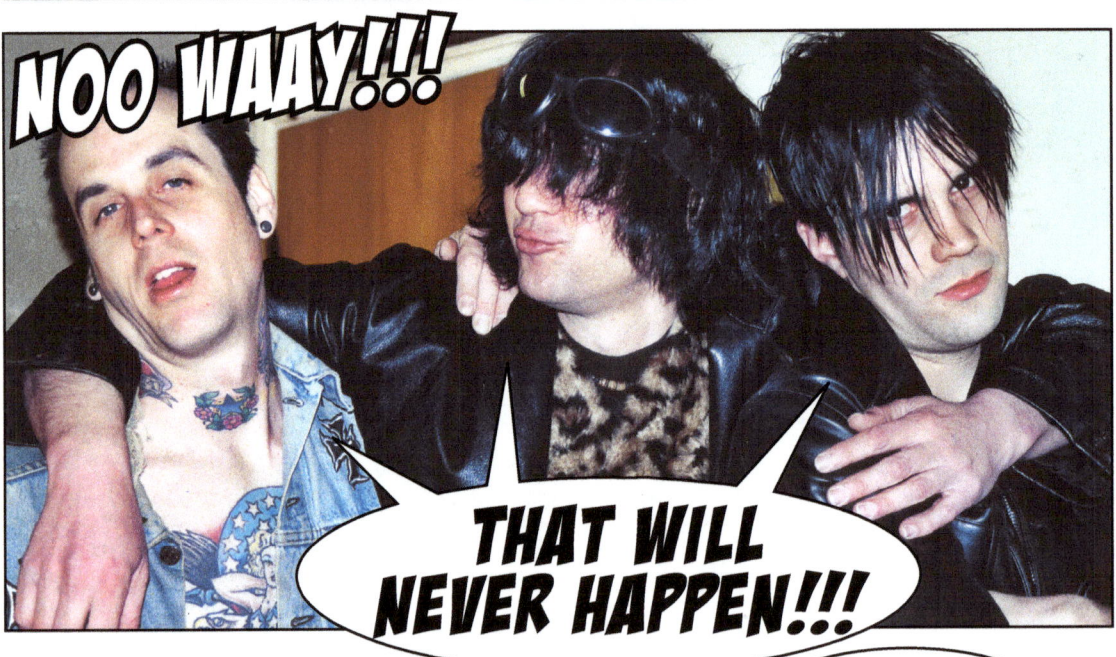

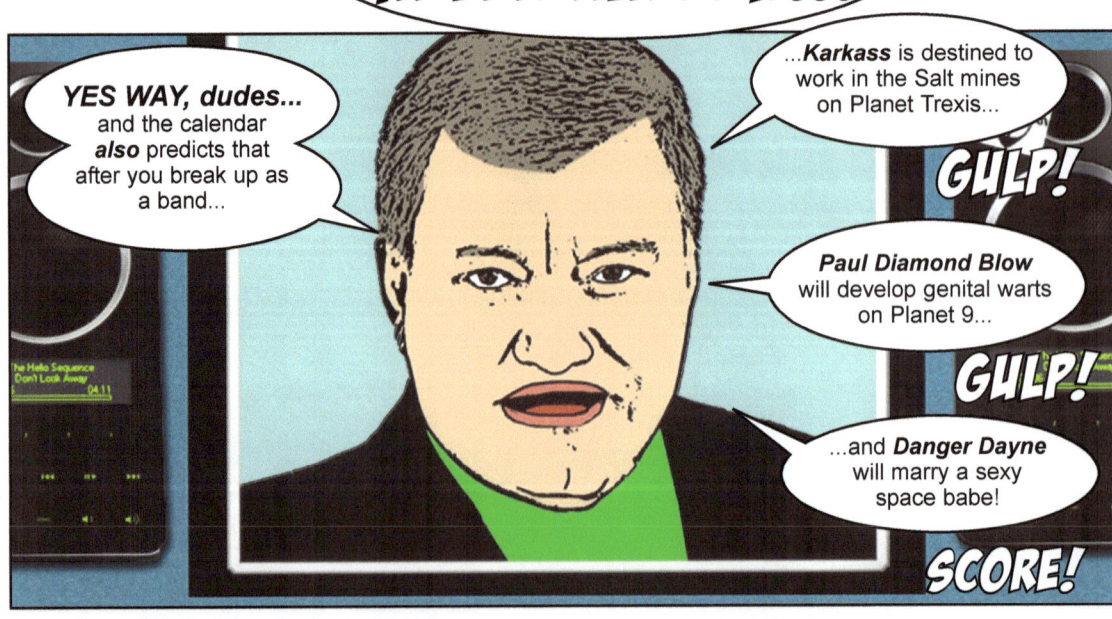

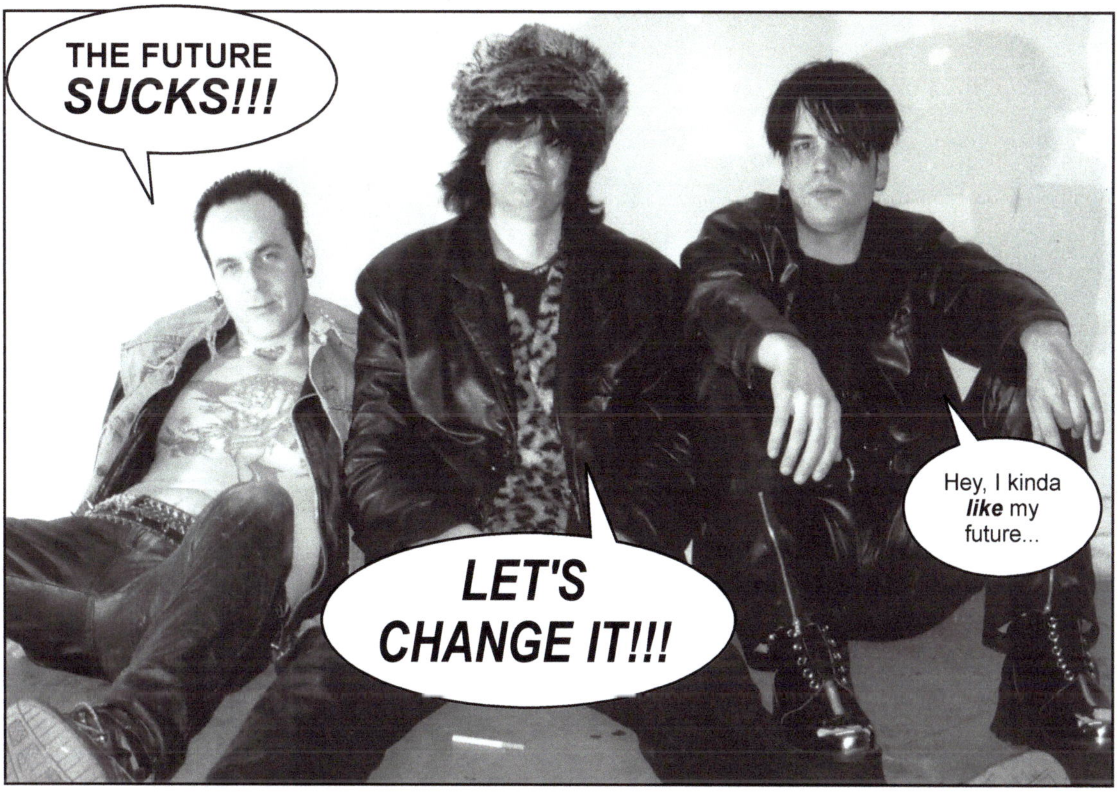

SOON... back at SPACE CRETINS headquarters...

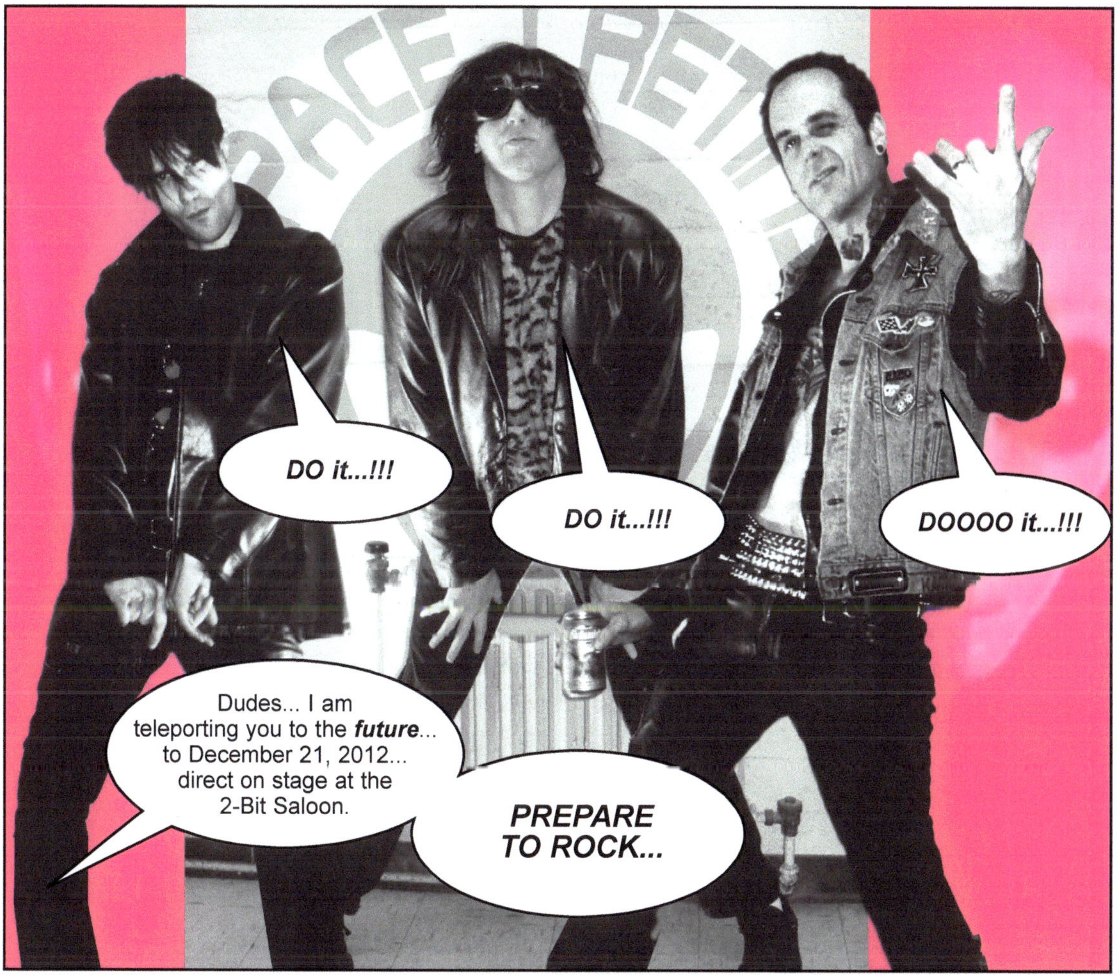

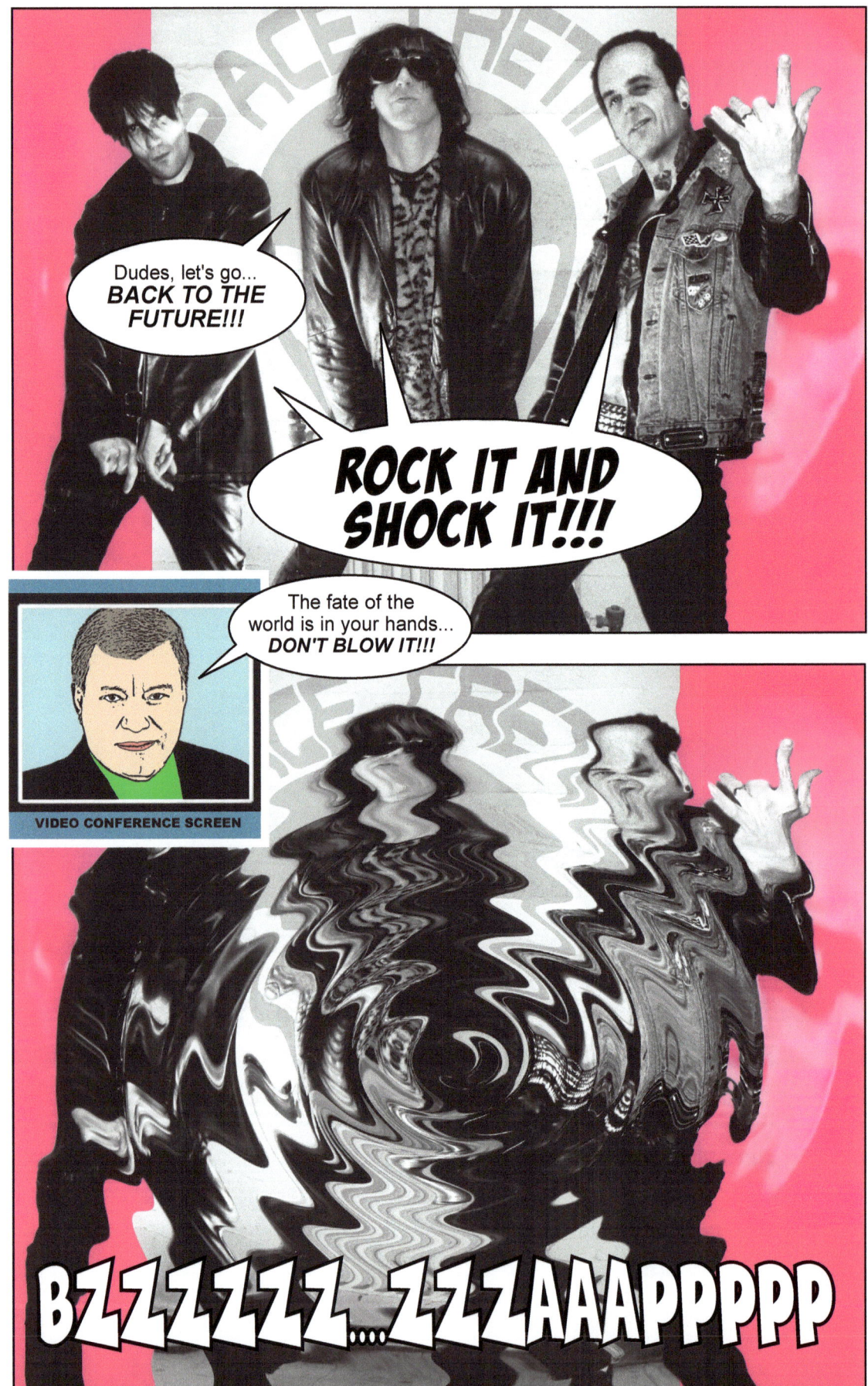

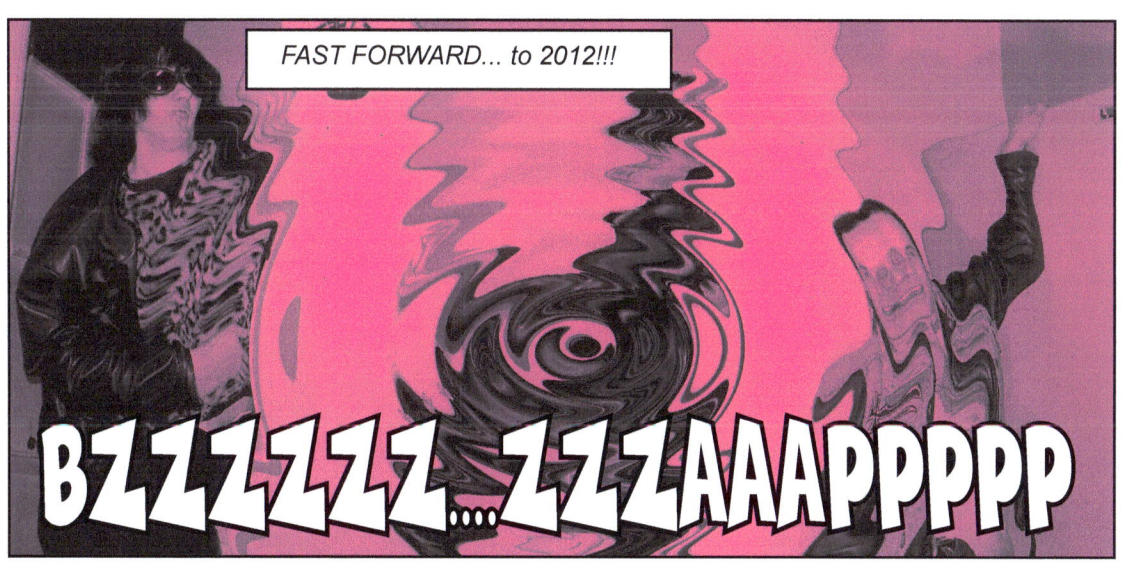

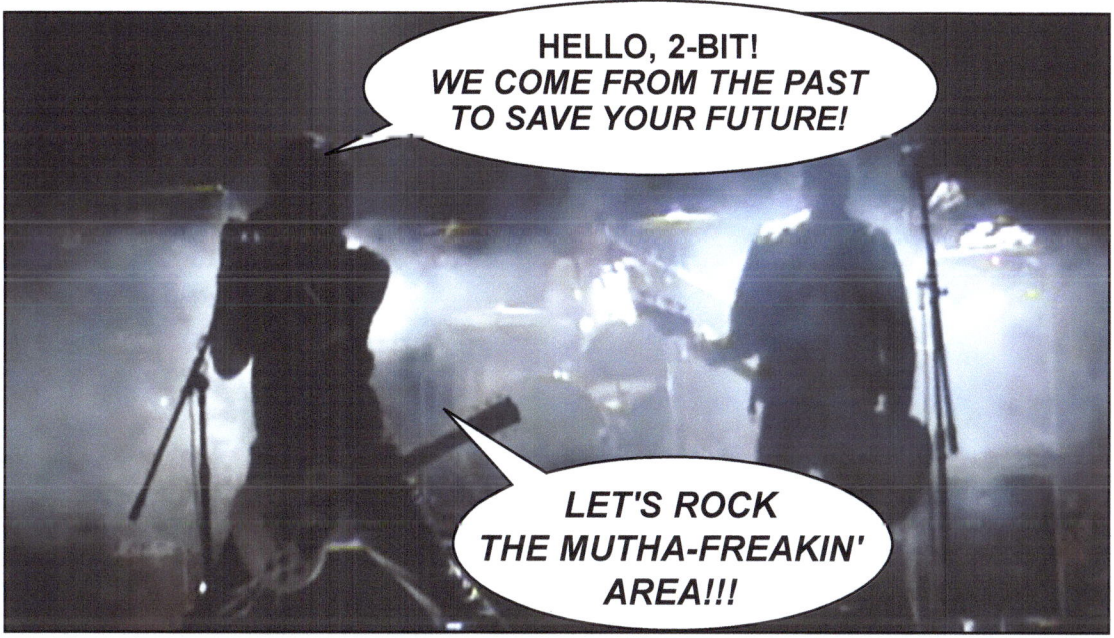

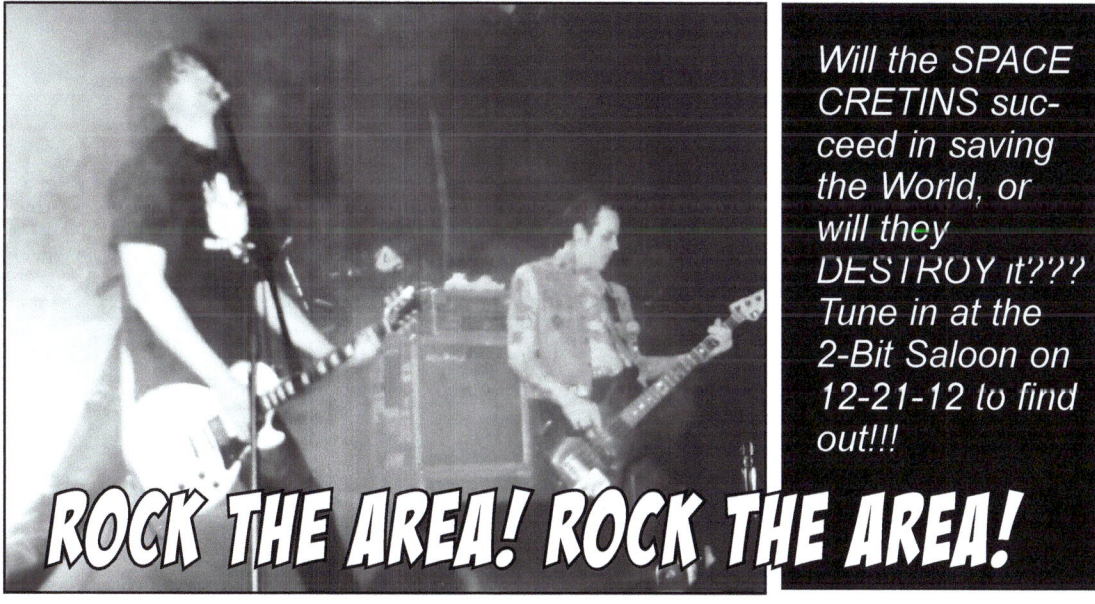

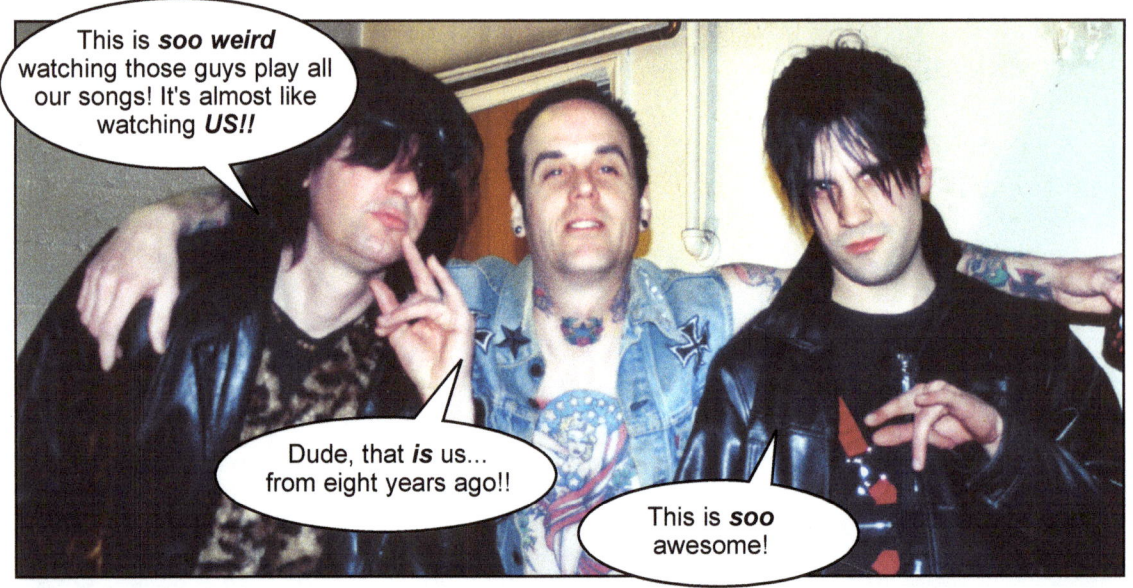

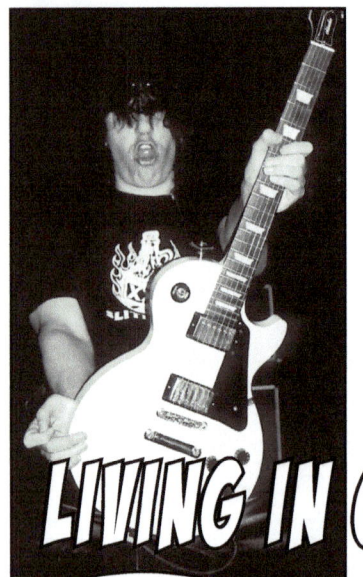
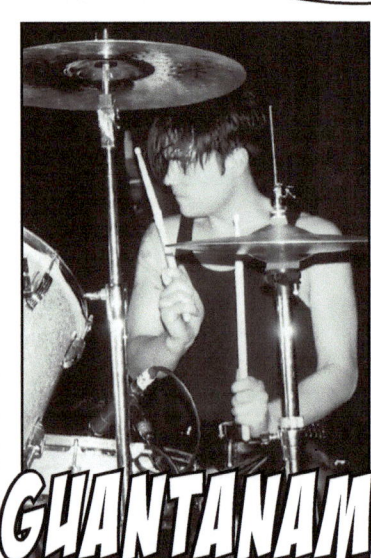
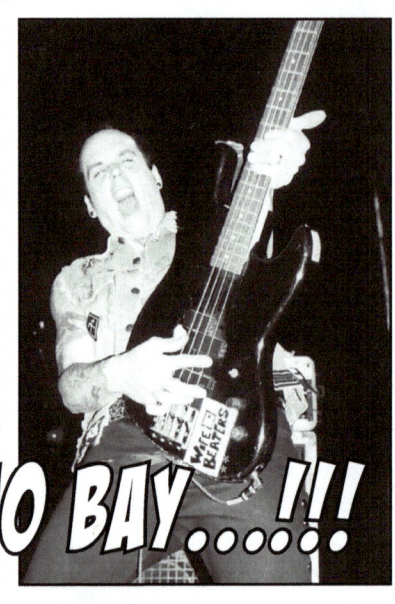

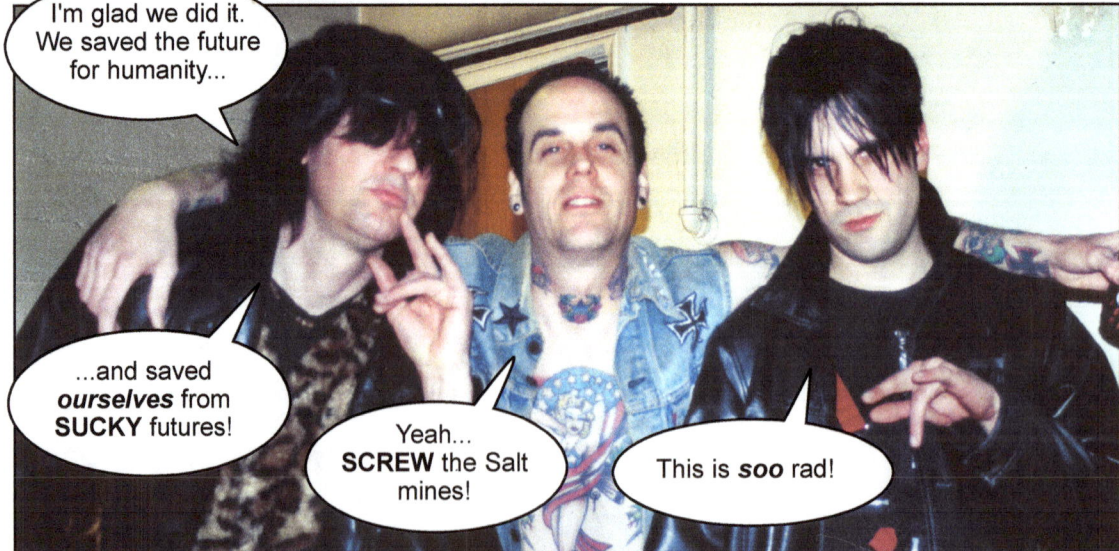

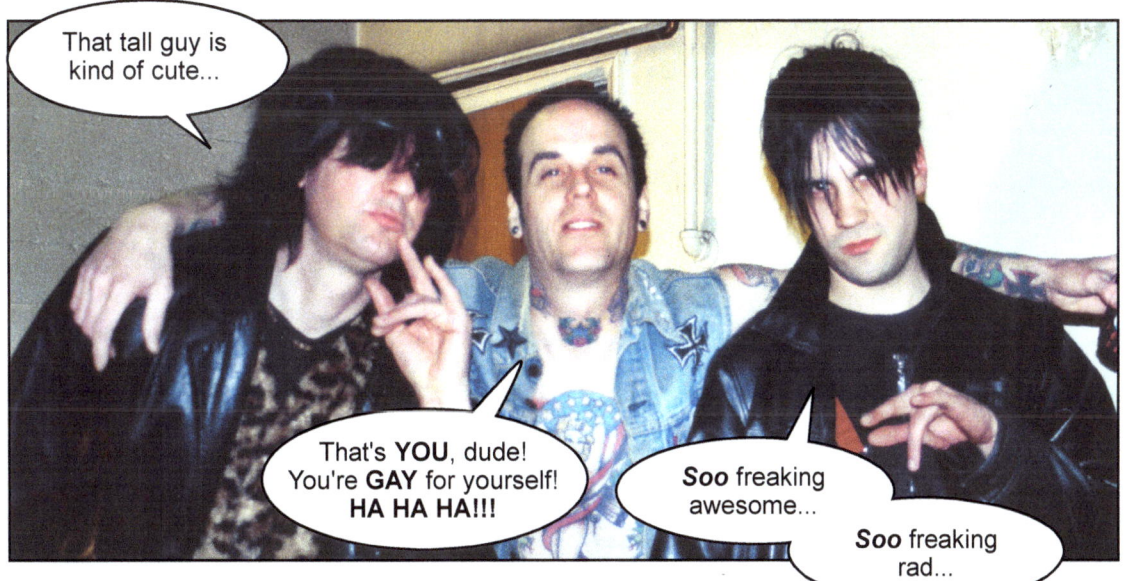

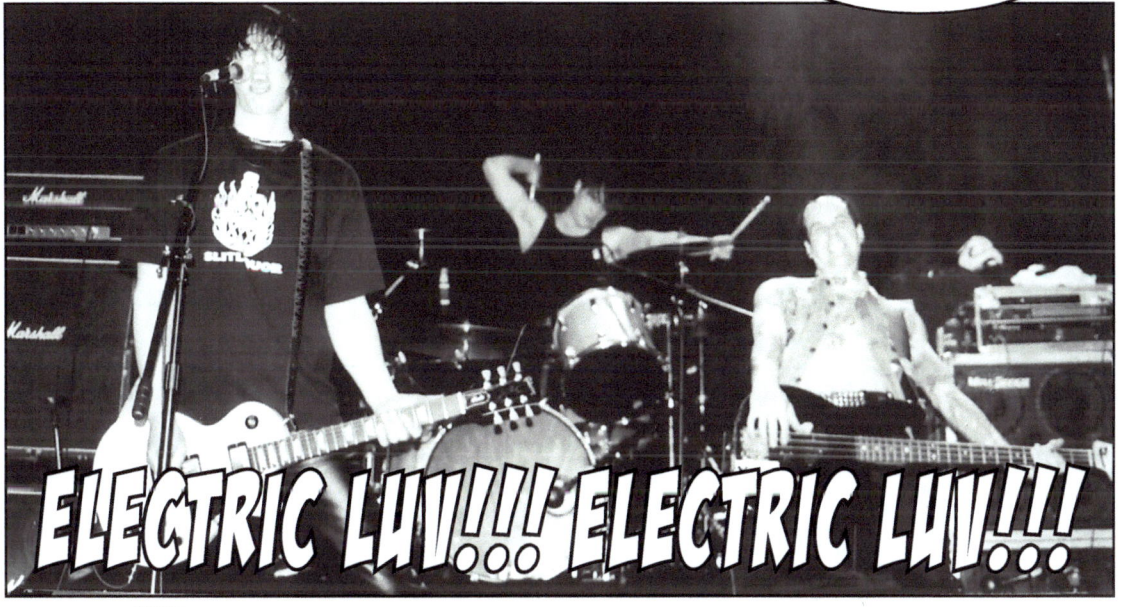

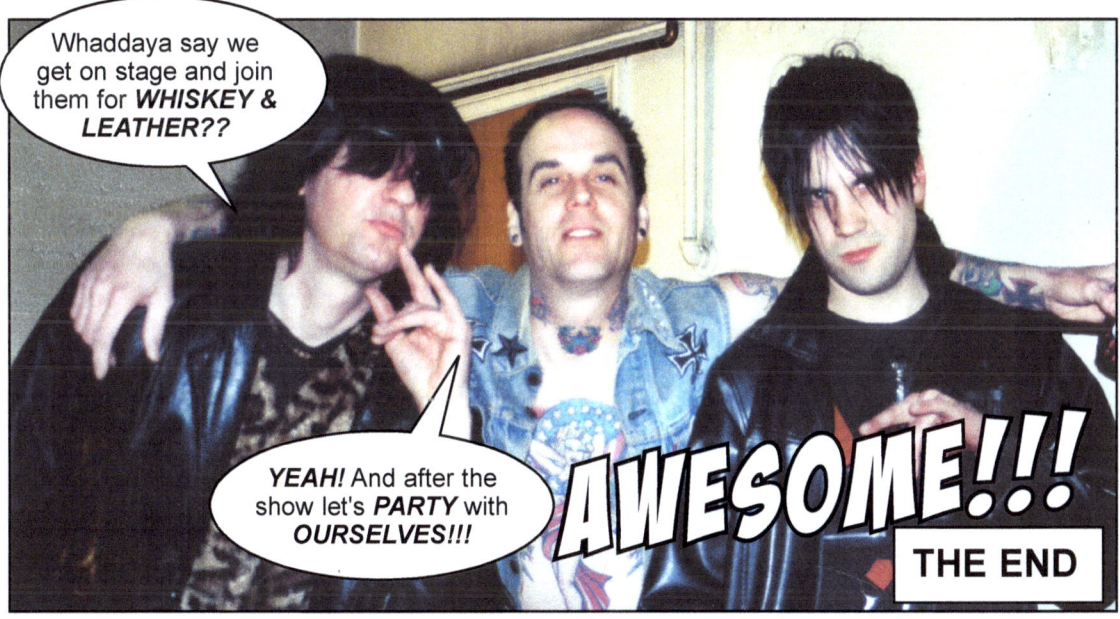

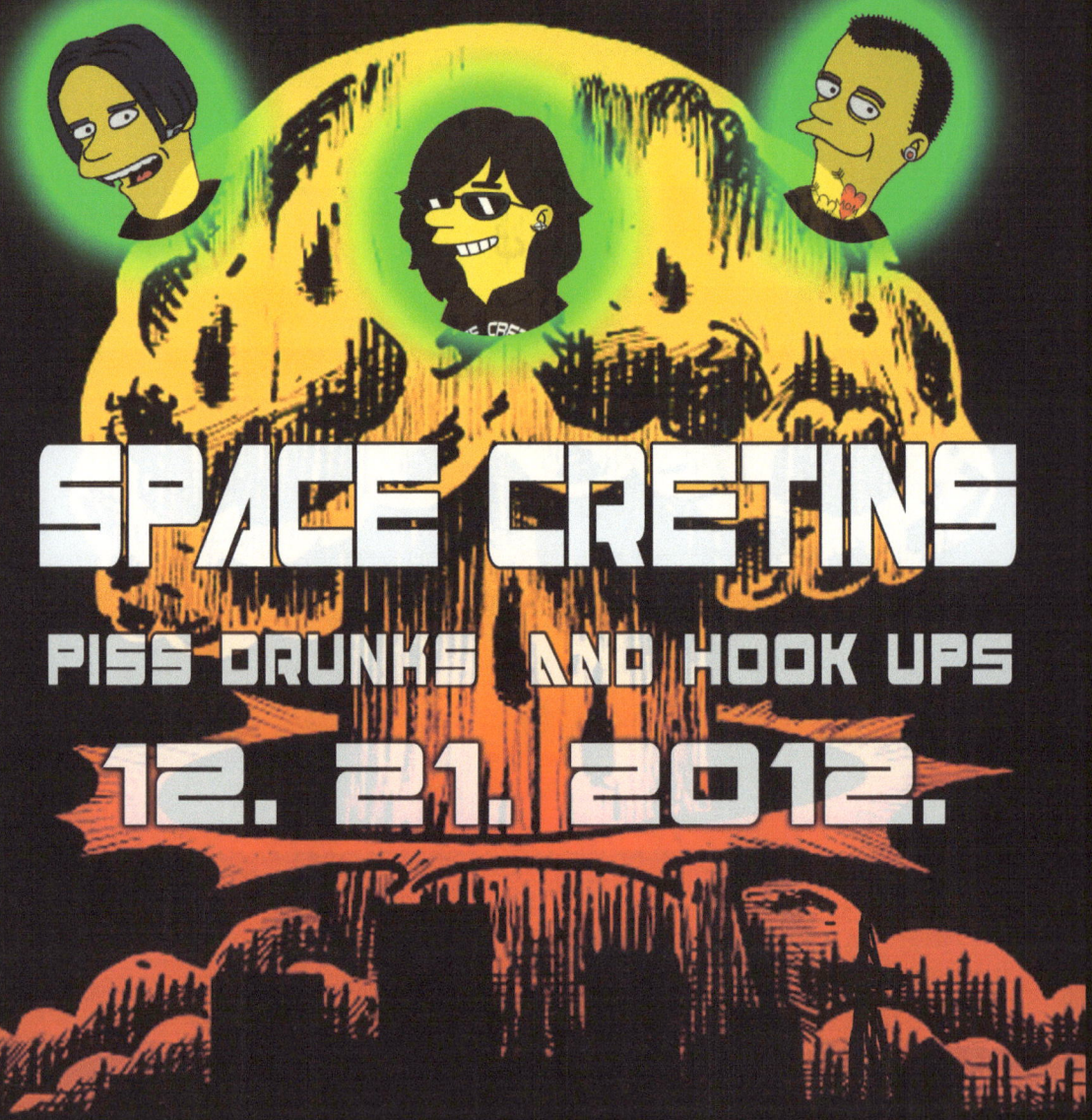

END OF THE WORLD PARTY WITH

SPACE CRETINS

PISS DRUNKS AND HOOK UPS

12. 21. 2012.

SPACE CRETINS REUNION WITH ORIGINAL LINEUP
PLAYING THE CD ROCET ROLL IN IT'S ENTIRETY

2 BIT SALOON

21 AND OVER   9PM   6.00

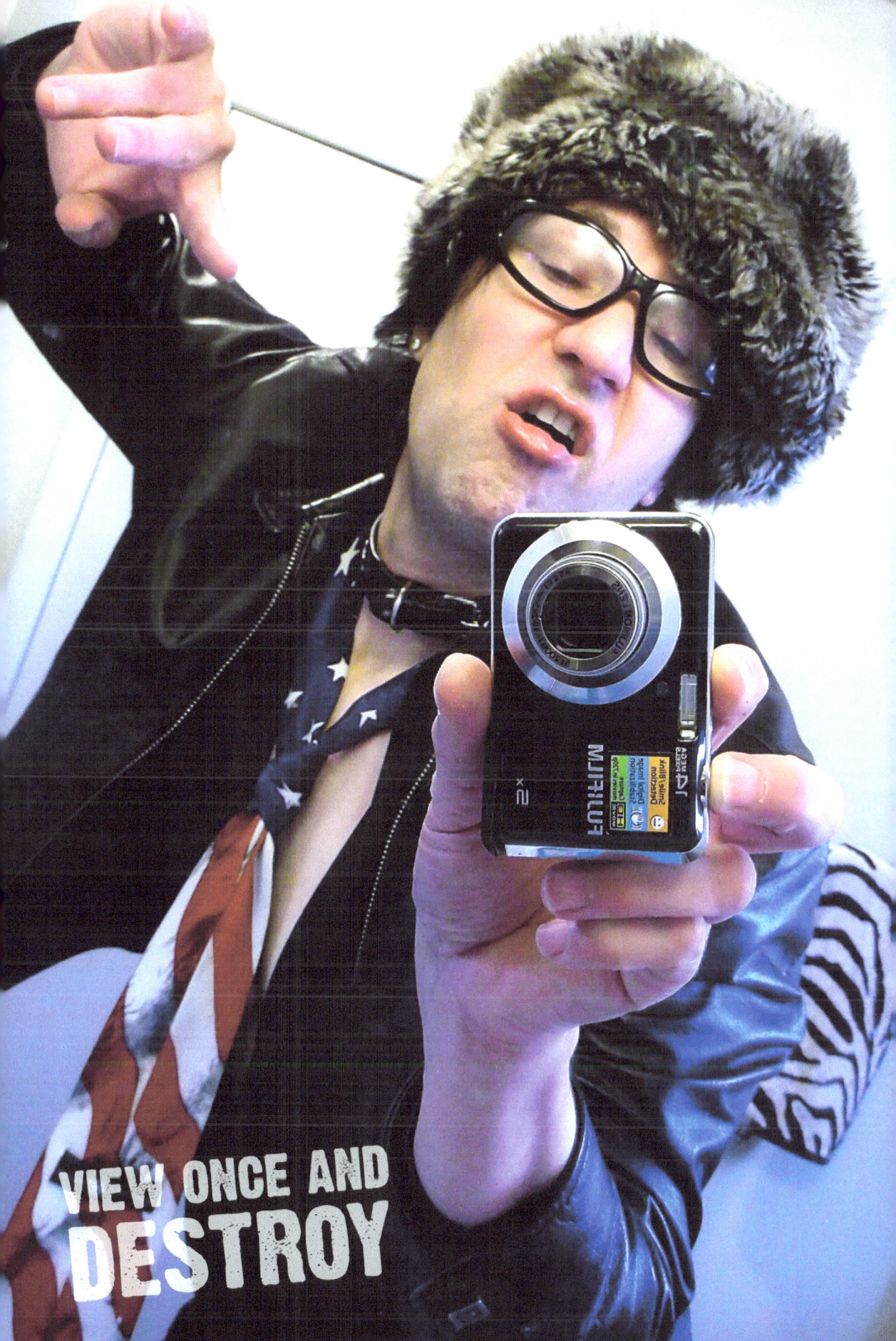

VIEW ONCE AND
DESTROY

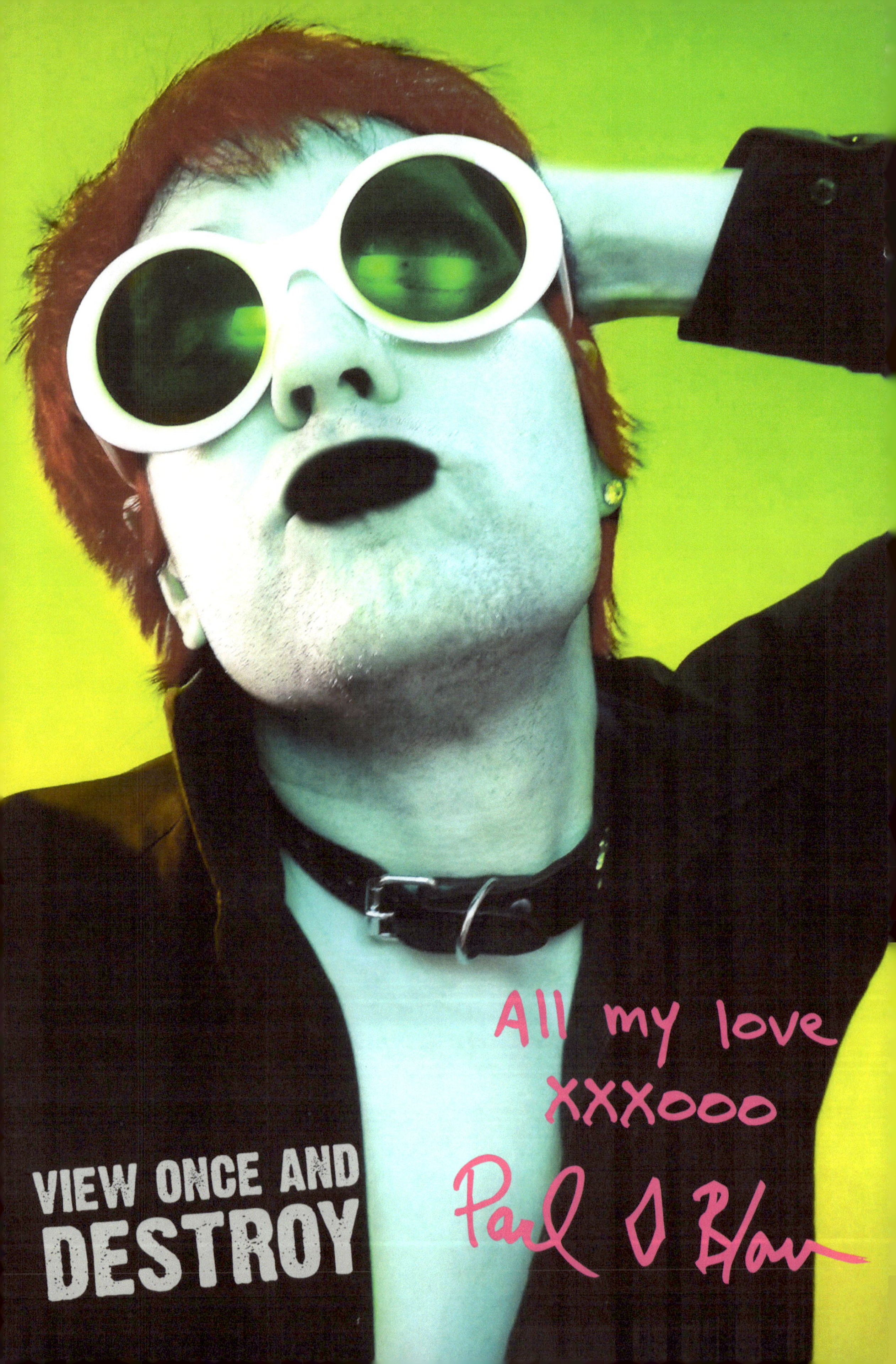

VIEW ONCE AND
DESTROY

All my love
xxxooo
Paul O B/av

If you enjoyed this book be sure to check out...

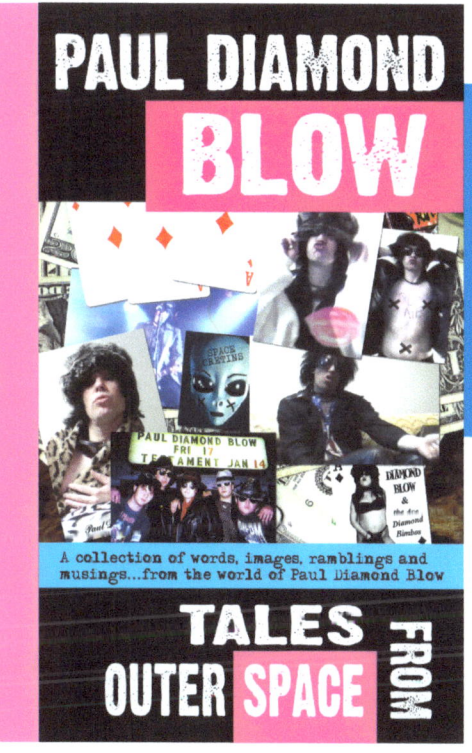

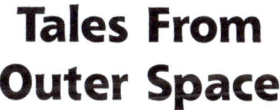

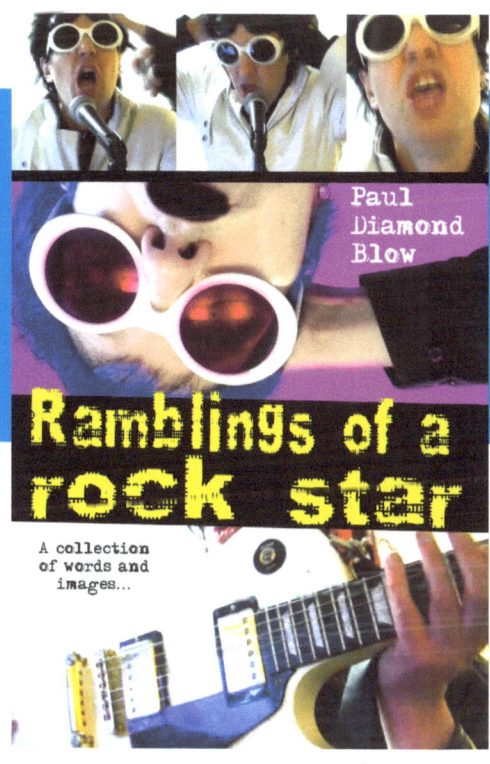

Tales From Outer Space

Rock'n'roll bands... kung fu... spoken word... myspace kidnappings... internet exorcisms... psychic channeling of dead rock stars... welcome to the world of Paul Diamond Blow. One part rock'n'roll advice, one part mad ramblings, and three parts sheer comedic genius, *Tales From Outer Space* will educate, entertain, stimulate and titillate you—not necessarily in that order.
204 pages $12.99

Ramblings of a Rock Star

A collection of poetry, song lyrics, spoken word, art, and random ramblings, once confined to obscure websites and cocktail napkins, and now published in book form for the masses to consume... direct from the rambling mind of rock'n'roller turned author, Paul Diamond Blow.
140 pages $12.99

Available on amazon.com and the PDB website (paulblow.tripod.com)

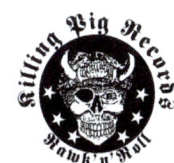

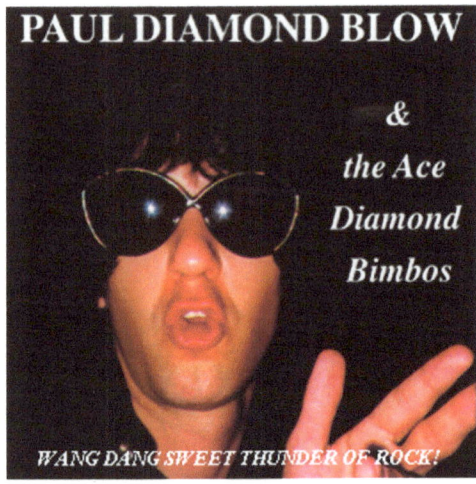
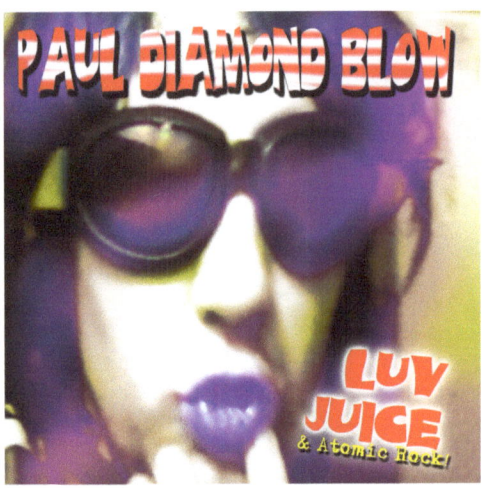
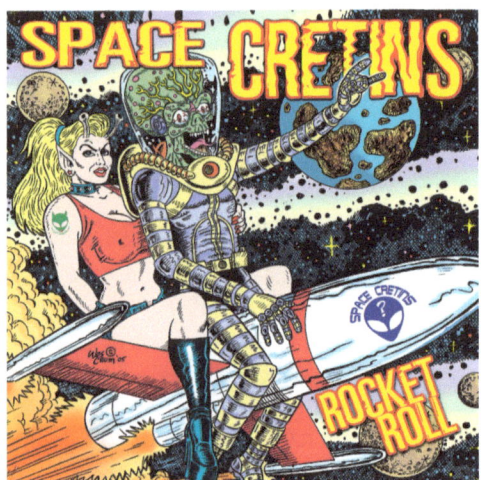
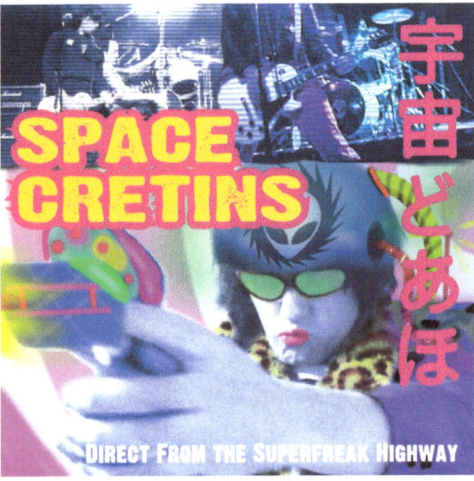
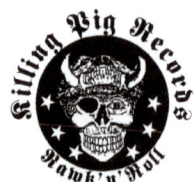